King Louis 15th

*Rumor has it that **Naomi** and **Roma** are direct descendants of King Louis XV Known as the Beloved King of France. Becoming King at the tender age of five, the King was by Phillippe II, Duke of Orleans until he was given full command of the throne at thirteen.*

At fifteen he married twenty-one-year-old Marie Leszczynska, daughter of Stanislaus I, the deposed King of Poland. During the mid-1700's and caused by one Of Frances conflicts, one Of the Kings offspring was secretly shipped Off to Canada to avoid assassination.

The ancestors of Louis Cozack Latterell are known to have settled in Quebec, Canada. The founder Of the Latterell family, Alexis Dubord dit LaTourelle, is believed. by some. to be the son of King Louis XV of France, in Claudia Dziuk's book *The Genealogy of the Latterell' Family" (1803-1933)

Naomi (1901-2005) was a Latterell and in marriage to Bernard (Ben) Jurek had two sons and daughter Roma (1930), As in most families, recipes were handed down from generation to generation.

This Cook Book is a culmination of the very things that are treasured throughout the ages in the form of gifts that sustain the very essence of life, love and kinship,

Roma presents these delicious recipes and hopes you enjoy and share them with your friends.
May God Bless.

Preface

The beginning of each section starts with a lined page for notes about that section.

If you try a recipe and you think there's too much or too little of an ingredient, make note of your change, so you can make it to your taste the next time you make it.

If a recipe needs to be cooked, fried or baked longer or at a higher or lower temperature.

If you find adding or taking away an ingredient, make the finished product more perfect to you or your family's taste.

Table of Contents

Appetizers_____4

Breads and Rolls_____17

Salads and Dressings_____34

Soups_____48

Meats_____55

Casseroles and Hotdishes ____66

Cakes and Frostings_____76

Pies _____95

Deserts_____109

Cookies Candies & Bars_____131

Pickles _____161

Miscellaneous _____169

Appetizers

_____

_____

_____

_____

_____

_____

_____

_____

Naomi
Herb Veggie Dip
from Aunt Phil

1 cup mayonnaise
1 cup sour cream
1 tablespoon minced onion
1-1/4 tablespoons parsley flakes
1-1/4 tablespoons dill weed
1/2 teaspoon curry powder
1/2 teaspoon garlic powder

Mix and serve with raw veggies

Per Serving (excluding unknown items):
514 Calories; 49g Fat (82.6% calories from fat);
9g Protein: 14g Carbohydrate; 1g Dietary Fiber; 102mg
Cholesterol; 132mg Sodium. Exchanges:
0 Grain (Starch); 1/2 Vegetable; 1/2 Non-Fat Milk;
911/2 Fat.

CORN FRITTERS

Ingredients:
1 cup all-purpose flour
1 teaspoon baking powder
1/2 teaspoon salt
2 tablespoons sugar
1 egg
1/3 cup milk
4 tablespoons maple syrup
1 tablespoon oil
1-2/3 cups fresh-cut sweet corn
Oil for frying
Directions:
Sift flour, measure next 3 ingredients.
Beat egg, add milk, maple syrup and oil, then flour
mixture and beat with spoon until smooth. Fold in
corn. Let stand 5-10 minutes while heating oil.
Fry at 360 deg. F (or med high heat on stove).
These are great with melted butter and/or
preserves.
Adding onion, garlic or cheese is a fabulous
touch.

Deep Fried Breaded Tomatoes'

Ingredients:
4 medium to large tomatoes' (sliced about 1/4 inch thick)
1 egg (beaten with a pinch of salt and pepper)
1/2 cup all-purpose flour
1/4 cup corn starch
1 tsp. baking powder
1/2 cup water
1 tbsp. water
1 tbsp. vegetable oil
1-1/2 cups canola oil
Directions:
Pour oil into a frying pan on medium heat.
Combine flour, corn starch, baking powder and salt on a dinner plate.
In a mixing bowl combine 1/2 cup water, 1 tbsp. water, beaten egg and tbsp. oil.
Dip tomato slices into mixture.
Place in oil in frying pan for 3 minutes both sides or until golden brown.
Serve with Ranch, Blue Cheese and Cucumber Dressing, Bar-B-Que Sauce, Ketchup, Horseradish and Cocktail Sauces.

Fried Cheese Balls

Deep fried mozzarella cheese, made with mozzarella cheese sticks or cubes and seasoned bread crumbs.

Ingredients:

1-pound Mozzarella cheese, cut into 3/4-to-1-inch sticks or cubes

2/3 cup all-purpose flour

1/3 tbsp. garlic powder

3 large eggs, beaten

3/4 cup Italian seasoned bread crumbs (If you use croutons place them in a plastic bag and use a rolling pin to crush)

vegetable shortening or oil, for frying

Directions:

In a deep fryer, frying pan with cover or deep Dutch oven, melt about 2 to 3 inches of oil or vegetable shortening over high heat; continue to heat until temperature reaches about 365 degrees.

Place the flour in a shallow bowl or pie plate. Beat the eggs in bowl. Place the seasoned bread crumbs in another shallow bowl or pie plate. One at a time, roll each mozzarella cube or stick in the flour – garlic powder mixture, dip in the eggs, then coat thoroughly with the bread crumbs. Set on a waxed paper-lined baking sheet.

Cook cubes or sticks until golden brown, about 3 minutes turning once after 1-1/2 minutes. Using a slotted spoon, transfer to paper towel-lined baking sheet and keep warm.

Utilize those fancy toothpicks you bought in each one to serve to your guests.

Deviled Egg Recipe
Ingredients:
6 eggs
1/4 cup mayonnaise
1 teaspoon yellow mustard
3/4 teaspoon white wine vinegar
pinch of salt
fresh ground black pepper
Directions:
Hard boil eggs, peeled and halved
Separate yokes and set white aside
Combine yokes and all other ingredients.
Mash with fork until mixed thoroughly.

(Green) Guacamole with egg yolk
(Red) Bacon Cheddar egg yolk red food coloring
(Yellow) Regular egg yolk
(Orange) Regular egg yolk (red & yellow) food coloring

You can try these other ingredients in the filling.
Garlic Cloves, Shrimp, Crab Meat, Smoked
Salmon, Olives, Onion, Capers, Bean Dip, Finely
Chopped Cooked Broccoli, Finely Chopped
Cooked or Raw Spinach, Any kind of Cheese,
Horseradish, Worcestershire, Any kind of
Mustard, Mushrooms, Cream Cheese, or Sour
Cream.

Cheese Jalapeno Poppers

Ingredients:
1 jar Jalapeno slices
Cubed cheese (1/2 x 1/2 x 1/4)
1 can of refried beans
2 tbsps. salsa
1/8 tsp. cumin
1/4 tbsp. chili powder
1/2 tbsp. cilantro
1 dash of Tabasco
1 egg (beaten on a dinner plate)
1 cup bread crumbs (on a dinner plate)
1-1/2 cups canola oil
Directions:
Place canola oil in a pan over medium heat.
Mix salsa, Tabasco, cumin, chili powder, cilantro
and refried beans in a bowl.
Sandwich a jalapeno slice with 2 cheese cubes.
Insert the jalapeno cheese sandwich into a dollop
of refried salsa mix cover the entire amount.
Roll the mixture ball in the egg then in the bread
crumbs.
Place in hot oil in frying pan turning once until
brown.

French Onion Soup Stuffed Mushrooms

Ingredients:
2 tablespoons butter
2 whole large onions, Halved and Sliced Thin
1/4 cup beef broth
7 dashes Worcestershire sauce
splash white wine
1/2 cup gruyere cheese, grated (can Use Swiss)
kosher salt
24 whole crimini mushrooms, Washed and Stems Removed
fresh parsley, minced
Directions:
In a medium skillet, melt 1 tablespoon butter over medium heat. Add onions and sauté for 15 to 20 minutes, stirring occasionally, until very soft. Splash in wine, broth, and Worcestershire. Cook for another 5 minutes, or until liquid is cooked down. Set aside.
Melt 1 tablespoon butter in a large skillet over medium heat. Throw in mushrooms and toss around for 2 minutes, just to start the cooking process. Sprinkle mushrooms with salt.
Place mushroom caps face down in a baking dish. Heap cavity with sautéed mushrooms, then sprinkle Gruyere over the top. Bake at 10 minutes on 325 degrees. Turn on broiler and broil for a couple of minutes, until the top of the Gruyere starts to bubble and slightly turn brown.
Sprinkle minced parsley over the top and serve.

Fruit Stuffed Tomato

Ingredients:
6 large tomato's
Apple (sliced)
Peach (sliced)
Mandarin orange
Kiwi (sliced)
Green grapes (seedless)
Strawberry (sliced)
Mango (sliced)
1/8 cup honey
3 cups Rhine wine
1/4 cup Miracle Whip or Mayonnaise
Directions:
Place the rest of the ingredients in the large bowl and let marinade 24 hours.
Cut tops off of tomato's and scoop out insides with a spoon.
Place tomato insides in the large bowl with other ingredients.
Drain bowl and fold in Miracle Whip or Mayonnaise
Spoon fruit mixture into hollowed tomatoes.
Don't forget to drink the liquid that was in the bowl (I think this is the best part)

Roma
Cocktail Meatballs

3 pounds hamburger - rolled in small balls.
Bake in oven about 1/2 hour.

Sauce:
1 cup catsup
1 cup chili sauce
1/2 cup tomato paste
1 teaspoon dry mustard
1/2 cup beef bullion
1/2 cup white sugar
2 teaspoons smoke
dash tabasco sauce

Hard Boiled Egg and Onion

Ingredients:
3 eggs (hard boiled and sliced)
1 medium onion (sliced)
2 tbsps. butter
2 tbsps. vinegar
1 tbsp. mustard
1/2 tbsp. cayenne flakes
1/8 tsp. garlic salt
1/2 tsp. caraway seeds
Directions:
Melt butter in medium sauce pan.
Stir in onion (simmer 4 to 5 minutes)
Add vinegar, mustard, cayenne, garlic salt and caraway.
Simmer an additional 4 to 5 minutes.
Spoon mixture over warm egg slices.

Pickled Beets Simple and Easy

Ingredients:
1 can of whole, sliced, diced or pieces.
(Approximately 14 oz.)
1/4 cup white sugar.
1/2 cup white vinegar.
1 tbsp. lemon juice.
Directions:
Place beets into a sauce pan and bring to a boil.
Stir in other ingredients.
Reduce heat and simmer for 5 to 6 minutes.
Let cool or eat hot.
You may add minced onion or garlic to taste.

Sweet Pickled Zucchini and or Yellow Squash

Ingredients:
9 cups water, divided
4 cups chunks peeled zucchini and crookneck or yellow squash
1 cup white vinegar
3 1/2 cups sugar
3 cinnamon sticks
1/2 teaspoon whole cloves
Directions:
In a large pot, bring 8 cups water and the squash to a boil over high heat. Boil for 15 to 20 minutes, or until the squash is fork-tender; drain and return rind to the pot.
Add the remaining 1 cup water, the vinegar, sugar, cinnamon sticks, and cloves; bring to a boil over high heat.
Reduce heat to medium, and cook 35 to 40 minutes, or until liquid has thickened slightly, stirring frequently.
Remove from heat and allow cooling. Transfer to an airtight container and chill overnight before serving or can in sterilized container.

Breads and Rolls

_____

_____

_____

_____

_____

_____

_____

_____

Naomi
Lemon Bread
Recipe from Aunt Sally (uncle Bob's wife)

1/2 cup oil
1 package lemon cake mix
1 package lemon pudding mix
4 eggs
1/4 cup poppyseed oil
1 cup lukewarm water
Mix all together except oil and eggs. Let
stand 10 min. Add oil and eggs and beat
10 minutes. Bake 40 min at 350^0

Yield: 2 loaves
Per Serving (excluding unknown items):
2081 Calories; 182g Fat (77.5% calories from fat); 22g
Protein; 96g Carbohydrate; Trace Dietary Fiber; 748mg
Cholesterol; 742mg Sodium. Exchanges: 3 Lean Meat;
34-1/2 Fat; 6-1/2 Other Carbohydrates.

Naomi
Zucchini Bread

3 eggs
3/4 cup cooking oil
1 cup sugar
3 cups flour
1 teaspoon salt
1 teaspoon soda
1-1/2 teaspoons baking powder
2 cups zucchini, grated
3 teaspoons vanilla
1-1/2 cups nuts, chopped
Beat eggs. Add oil and sugar. Sift together dry ingredients. Add zucchini and flour mixture alternately. Beat well.
Stir in vanilla and nuts. Bake in greased pans 1 hr at 350^0
Yield: 2 loaves
Per Serving (excluding unknown items):
5171 Calories; 301g Fat (51.4% calories from fat); 94g Protein; 546g Carbohydrate; 35g Dietary Fiber; 561mg Cholesterol; 3070mg Sodium. Exchanges: 21-1/2 Grain (Starch); 6 Lean Meat; 1 Vegetable; 55-1/2 Fat; 13-1/2 Other Carbohydrates.

Naomi
Orange Bread
This recipe comes from Bernelda Kalkman-Veranth

4 oranges
1 cup sugar
1/2 cup water
2 eggs, beaten
1 cup milk
2 tablespoons butter
3 cups flour
1 teaspoon soda
2 teaspoons baking powder

Boil the rind of the oranges in salt water until tender. Scrape out white and discard. Grind the orange peel. Add sugar and water to peel and boil until syrupy. Cool. Beat together the rest of the ingredients and then add syrup. Let rise. Bake 1 hr at 350^0.

Yield: 2 loaves
Per serving (excluding unknown items):
2874 Calories; 44g Fat (13.7% calories from fat); 63g Protein; 562g Carbohydrate; 23g Dietary Fiber; 469mg Cholesterol; 1453mg Sodium. Exchanges: 19 Grain (Starch); 1-1/2 Lean

Irish Soda Bread
This recipe came from Bernelda Kalkman-Veranth, Grandma Jurek's neighbor.

4 cups sifted all-purpose flour
1/3 cup sugar
2 teaspoons salt
1-1/2 teaspoons soda
1 tablespoon caraway seed, crushed in hands
1/2 cup currants or raisins
1-1/2 cups sour milk or buttermilk

Sift flour with sugar, salt and soda in large bowl. Add caraway seed and raisins. Make a well in center and add other ingredients. Add sour milk. Mix 'til all are moistened and cling together. Tum on floured board and knead until smooth and not sticky, 2-3 min. Shape into loaf and bake at 350^0 for 55 min.
Yield: 1 loaf

Naomi
Rhubarb Nut Bread

1-1/2 cups brown sugar
2/3 cup salad oil
1 egg
1 cup sour milk (add 1 tsp vinegar to 1 c milk)
1 teaspoon salt, soda & vanilla
2-1/2 cups flour
1-1/2 cups fresh rhubarb, diced
1/2 cup nuts, chopped

Mix together all ingredients and pour into two greased loaf pans and sprinkle over the batter a mixture of 1/2 cup sugar and 1 tbsp butter. Bake at 325^0 about 60 min. Do Not Overbake!

Yield: 1 loaf
Per Serving (excluding unknown items):
312 Calories; 16g Fat (45.7% calories from fat);
4g Protein; 39g Carbohydrate; 1g Dietary Fiber; 16mg Cholesterol; 13mg Sodium. Exchanges:
1-1/2 Grain (Starch); 0 Lean Meat; 3 Fat; 1 Other Carbohydrates.

Naomi
Nut Bread

4 cups flour
4 teaspoons baking powder
1 cup sugar
1 cup raisins
1 cup nuts
1 dash salt
1/2 cup lard
2 eggs
sweet milk to make a stiff batter

Let raise 30 minutes. Bake 45 min 350^0.
Yield: 2 loaves
Per Serving (excluding unknown items):
414 Calories; 16g Fat (35.0% calories from fat);
8g Protein; 61g Carbohydrate; 3g Dietary Fiber; 39mg
Cholesterol; 198mg Sodium. Exchanges:
2 Grain (Starch); 1/2 Lean Meat; 1/2 Fruit; 3 Fat;
1 Other Carbohydrates.

Roma
Lemonade Bread

1/3 cup thawed lemonade concentrate + 1 Tbsp
1/2 cup vegetable oil
1 cup sugar
2 eggs
1-1/2 cups flour
2 teaspoons baking powder
1/2 cup milk

Combine all ingredients except 1/3 cup lemonade concentrate. Blend well. Pour batter into greased 9"x 5" pan. Bake at 350^0 for 50-60 min. Loosen bread from edges of pan. Pour 1/3 cup concentrate over bread. Cool; remove from pan.

Yield: I loaf
Per Serving (excluding unknown items);
2631 Calories; 124g Fat (41.9% calories from fat); 34g Protein; 352g Carbohydrate; 5g Dietary Fiber; 391mg Cholesterol; 1152mg Sodium. Exchanges:
9-1/2 Grain (Starch); 1-1/2 Lean Meat; 1/2 Non-Fat Milk; 23-1/2 Fat; 13-1/2 Other Carbohydrates.

Roma
Dad's Crockpot Bread

1/2 cup brown rice flour
1-1/2 cups white rice flour
1/2 cup corn starch
1/2 cup sugar (or sugar substitute)
1 teaspoon salt
2-1/2 teaspoons baking powder
2 teaspoons gelatin in I tbsp water
2 tablespoons olive oil
2 egg yolks
1 cup plain yogurt
3/4 cup milk

Mix together all ingredients. Put in pan in crockpot and cook on high until toothpick comes out clean.
Yield: 1 loaf
Per Serving (excluding unknown items):
1781 Calories; 57g Fat (29.0% calories from fat); 40g Protein; 274g Carbohydrate; 9g Dietary Fiber; 481mg Cholesterol; 3575mg Sodium. Exchanges: 16-1/2 Grain (Starch); 1/2 Lean Meat; 1-1/2 Non-Fat Milk; 10 Fat; 1 Other Carbohydrate

Mildred
Oatmeal Bread
This is the best ever
Ingredients:
2 cakes yeast
1/4 cup warm water
1 teaspoon sugar
2 cups boiling water
1 cup oatmeal
1/4 cup shortening
1 tablespoon salt
1/2 cup dark molasses
5 -1/2 cups flour
Directions:

Mix together yeast, 1/4 c water and sugar. Set aside. Stir boiling water, oatmeal, Shortening, salt and molasses until shortening melts, then cool to lukewarm. Add yeast mixture. Mix in flour. Let rise until double in bulk. Form into loaves, let rise again. Bake at 350^0 for 45-50 min.

Yield: 2 loaves
Per Serving (excluding unknown items):
188 Calories; 3g Fat (15.4% calories from fat);
4g Protein; 35g Carbohydrate; 2g Dietary Fiber; 0mg
Cholesterol; 325mg Sodium. Exchanges:
2 Grain (Starch); 0 Lean Meat; 1/2 Fat; 1/2 Other
Carbohydrates.

Roma
Corn Bread

1 cup corn meal
1 cup milk
1 cup cream style corn
1/2 cup oil
2 eggs
1 teaspoon salt
1 teaspoon baking powder
onions and cheese to taste

Mix all ingredients and bake at 350^0 for 1
hour. Serving Ideas: I serve it with butter and
syrup, or as a side with a meal
Yield: 1 loaf
Per Serving (excluding unknown items):
208 Calories; 21g Fat (89.7% calories from fat);
3g Protein; 2g Carbohydrate; 0g Dietary Fiber; 68mg
Cholesterol; 475mg Sodium. Exchanges:
1/2 Lean Meat; 0 Non-Fat Milk; 4 Fat; 0 Other
Carbohydrates.

Roma
Apricot Nut Bread

3 cups flour
1 cup sugar
1 tablespoon baking powder
1/2 teaspoon salt
1/4 teaspoon soda
1 egg, beaten
1-2/3 cups milk
1/4 cup oil
3/4 cup nuts
2 teaspoons orange rind, grated
1 cup dried apricots, finely chopped

Mix together flour, sugar, baking powder, soda and salt. Combine egg, milk and oil. Mix together. Add nuts, orange rind and apricots. Place in 4 small pans (soup cans will do). Bake at 350⁰ for 35-40 min.

Yield: 4 small loaves
Per Serving (excluding unknown items):
3914 Calories; 137g Fat (30.7% calories from fat); 80g Protein; 613g Carbohydrate;
33g Dietary Fiber; 242mg Cholesterol; 2818mg Sodium. Exchanges: 20 Grain (Starch); 2-1/2 Lean Meat; 5-1/2 Fruit; 1-1/2 Non-Fat Milk; 24-1/2 Fat; 13-1/2 Other Carbohydrates

Roma
Banana Bread

1/2 cup oil
2 eggs
1 cup sugar
3 bananas
1/4 teaspoon salt
2-1/2 cups flour
1/2 cups cold water
1 teaspoon soda
1/2 cup nuts (optional)
1 teaspoon baking powder

Mix together. Bake at 350^0 for 1 hour.

Roma
Rice Bread

2-1/2 cups rice flour
3/4 cup corn starch
3 tablespoons instant mashed potatoes
3 teaspoons baking powder
2 tablespoons gelatin
1 teaspoon salt

Mix dry ingredients. Add 3 eggs, 1-1/4 cup buttermilk, 1/4 cup oil, 1 cup cottage cheese. Beat until creamy. Bake in small tins for 55 minutes at 350^0.

Naomi
Doughnuts
from Aunt Belle

1 cup buttermilk
3 egg yolks
1 cup flour
1 cup sugar
1/2 teaspoon soda
1/2 teaspoon baking powder
1/2 teaspoon nutmeg

Beat egg yolks and buttermilk together.
Sift dry ingredients together and mix into
egg yolk mixture. Add enough flour to
handle. Roll and cut into doughnuts. Fry.
Yield: 24 servings
Per Serving (excluding unknown items):
63 Calories; 1g Fat (11.3% calories from fat);
1g Protein; 13g Carbohydrate; Trace Dietary Fiber;
27mg Cholesterol; 22mg Sodium. Exchanges:
1/2 Grain (Starch); Lean Meat; 0 Non-Fat Milk;
0 Fat; 1/2 Other Carbohydrates.

Roma
Mini Caramel Rolls

2 loaves frozen bread dough, thawed
1/2 cup butter
3/4 cup brown sugar
1 package vanilla pudding mix, cooked not instant

Form about 35 one-inch balls from one loaf bread dough; place in buttered 9"x13" baking pan. Melt butter and sugar; stir in dry pudding mix; cool. Pour over bread dough balls. Repeat making 1" balls from second loaf. Place on top of caramel mixture. Let rise until double in bulk (about 2 hrs.) Bake at 350^0 for 30-40 min. Turn onto foil lined cookie sheet.
Yield: 10 servings
Per Serving (excluding unknown items):
413 Calories; 13g Fat (28.6% calories from fat);
9g Protein; 63g Carbohydrate; 4g Dietary Fiber; 25mg Cholesterol; 749mg Sodium. Exchanges:
1/2 Grain (Starch); 2 Fat; 1-1/2 Other Carbohydrates.

Naomi
Galoot (Bread Dumpling)
Mom frequently gave me this for lunch.

1 loaf bread dough

Have bread ready to put into pans. Divide into pancake size pieces and fry in deep fat on both sides. Sprinkle with butter and sugar or pancake syrup.

Delicious when boiled as a dumpling with pork, beef or chicken and gravy.

Per Serving (excluding unknown items):
144 Calories; 6g Fat (37.8% calories from fat);
3g Protein; 20g Carbohydrate; 1g Dietary Fiber;
0mg Cholesterol; 502mg Sodium. Exchanges:
1-1/2 Grain (starch); 1-1/2 Fat.

Salads and Dressings

_____

_____

_____

_____

_____

_____

_____

_____

Naomi
Sauerkraut Salad
from Aunt Belle

1 can sauerkraut, drained
1/2 bottle pimiento
1 green pepper
1 stalk celery, diced
1 smidgen onion (or chives)
3/4 cup sugar
1/4 cup water
1/4 cup vinegar
1/8 cup oil

Cut sauerkraut into small pieces with a scissors. Mix water, vinegar and oil and pour over mixture of other ingredients

Per Serving (excluding unknown items):
995 Calories; 37g Fat (32.0% calories from fat);
4g Protein; 173g Carbohydrate; 9g Dietary Fiber; 0mg
Cholesterol; 1602mg Sodium. Exchanges:
3-1/2 vegetable; 7-1/2 Fat 10-1/2 Other Carbohydrates

Naomi
Gelatin Salad
Excellent for Xmas

3 cups miniature marshmallows
1 cup crushed pineapple, drained
1/2 a pint whipped cream
1 package green gelatin
1 package red gelatin
3 cups water, divided

Prepare separately in shallow pans (square) the two Jellos, each with 1-1/2 cups of boiling water. Chill until set. Cut into squares and mix with the other ingredients. Serve

Per Serving (excluding unknown items):
1290 Calories; 88g Fat (59.7% calories from fat); 7g Protein; 127g Carbohydrate; 2g Dietary Fiber; 326mg Cholesterol; 159mg Sodium. Exchanges: 2-1/2 Fruit; 1/2 Non-Fat Milk; 17-1/2 Fat; 4-1/2 Other Carbohydrates.

Naomi
Frozen Cole Slaw

1 med head cabbage, coarsely chopped
1 or more carrots, finely shredded
1/4 cup pimiento, chopped
1 teaspoon salt.
1/4 cup onion, chopped

DRESSING
1 cup vinegar
2 cups sugar
1/4 cup water
1 teaspoon celery seed
1 teaspoon mustard seed

Mix salt and cabbage and let stand 1 hour. Boil dressing ingredients 1 min. and let cool. Squeeze extra juice from cabbage, add other ingredients and dressing. Freeze. Thaw before serving.

Per Serving (excluding unknown items):
1676 Calories; 2g Fat (1.0% calories from fat);
4g Protein; 432g Carbohydrate; 5g Dietary Fiber; 0mg
Cholesterol: 2186mg Sodium. Exchanges:
0 Grain (Starch); 0 Lean Meat; 3 Vegetable;
0 Fat; 28 Other Carbohydrates.

Naomi
Tuna Salad

1 can tuna
1 stalk celery
1 can crushed pineapple
1 smidgen slivered cheese

Mix tuna, celery and pineapple together with
mayonnaise dressing. Serve in lettuce cups.
Yield: 4 servings
Per Serving (excluding unknown items):
100 Calories; 2g Fat (19, 1% calories from fat);
10g Protein; 10g Carbohydrate; 1g Dietary Fiber; 16mg
Cholesterol; 26mg Sodium. Exchanges:
1-1/2 Lean Meat; 0 Vegetable; 1/2 Fruit.

Naomi
Cottage Cheese Salad
How Simple

1 small size cottage cheese
1 small size can crushed pineapple,
drained
1 small size carton whip cream
1 package orange gelatin

Mix together cottage cheese, pineapple and
Cool Whip. Sprinkle dry gelatin powder over
the top and let stand overnight.

Per Serving (excluding unknown items):
363 Calories; 5g Fat (12.4% calories from fat);
32g Protein; 48g Carbohydrate; 2g Dietary Fiber; 19mg
Cholesterol; 923mg Sodium. Exchanges:
4-1/2 Lean Meat; 2-1/2 Fruit; 0 Fat; 0 Other
Carbohydrates

Roma
Veggie Salad

1 package frozen mixed vegetables
1 can kidney beans
celery
green pepper
onion

Dressing: Combine in pot, boil and stir 2 mins
1/4 cup sugar
1 tablespoon flour
salt and pepper
1/2 cup vinegar
1 tablespoon mustard

Put in a jar and shake well or put in
blender.

This recipe came from Dad's Aunt Edith
(married to Uncle Bill) who was the
head chef at the Ace for many years.
Yield: 1 3/4 cups
Per Serving (excluding unknown items):
1246 Calories; 73g Fat (50.8% calories from fat);
4g Protein; 157g Carbohydrate; 4g Dietary Fiber;
0mg Cholesterol; 4034mg Sodium. Exchanges:
1-1/2 Vegetable; 14-1/2 Fat; 10 Other Carbohydrates.

Naomi
Dandelion Salad
A Grandma Specialty

Wash enough dandelions for four persons.
Put into a bowl and add two chopped hard-
boiled eggs. In a skillet, fry 1/2 a pound
minced bacon. When done, take the skillet
from the heat and add to it 1/3 cup cider
vinegar and quickly pour over greens. Season
with salt and pepper.
Per Serving (excluding unknown items): 0 Calories; 0g
Fat (0.0% calories from fat); 0g Protein:
0g Carbohydrate; 0g Dietary Fiber;
0mg Cholesterol; 0mg Sodium. Exchanges:

Naomi
Cucumber Salad
from Dick's Bunny

1 package lime gelatin
3/4 cup boiling water
1 cup cottage cheese
2 teaspoons lemon juice
1 medium cucumber, diced
1 teaspoon onion, grated
1/2 cup celery, diced
1/3 cup walnuts, finely chopped

Mix gelatin and boiling water. Let cool. Add remaining ingredients and refrigerate until set. Serve on lettuce leaf.

Yield: 6 servings
Per Serving (excluding unknown items):
85 Calories; 5g Fat (48.2% calories from fat);
7g Protein; 4g Carbohydrate; 1g Dietary Fiber;
3mg Cholesterol; 164mg Sodium. Exchanges:
0 Grain (Starch); 1 Lean Meat; 1/2 Vegetable;
0 Fruit; 1/2 Fat.

Roma
Chinese Cabbage Salad
From Suzy

1 large head of cabbage, shredded
5 green onions, chopped
1/2 cup butter
2 packages ramen noodles, crunched
1 small pkg slivered almonds
1/2 cup sesame seeds
DRESSING
1 cup oil
112 cup cider vinegar
2 teaspoons soy sauce
1/2 cup sugar

Brown ramen noodles, sesame seeds and
almonds in the 1/2 cup butter, and cool. Mix
shredded cabbage and onions. Put dressing
ingredients in a jar and shake. Pour over cabbage and
onions that have been mixed with the noodle/nut
mixture.
Serving Ideas: I have never failed to be asked for the
recipe when I take this to a pot-luck. You can make this
ahead of time, just do not mix together until about 20
min before eating.
Per Serving (excluding unknown items):
3851 Calories; 332g Fat (73.9% calories from fat); 57g
Protein; 207g Carbohydrate; 4lg Dietary Fiber; 0mg
Cholesterol; 886mg Sodium.

Naomi
Wild Rice Salad

2 cups cooked wild rice
2 large apples
1 tablespoon lemon juice
2 tablespoons brown sugar
2 stalks celery, diced
1/3 cup mayonnaise
1/2 cup sour cream

Mix all and serve chilled
Per Serving (excluding unknown items):
825 Calories; 26g Fat (27.4% calories from fat);
18g Protein; 139g Carbohydrate; 15g Dietary Fiber;
51mg Cholesterol; 148mg Sodium. Exchanges:
4-1/2 Grain (Starch); 1/2 Vegetable; 3 Fruit;
1/2 Non-Fat Milk; 5 Fat; 1 Other Carbohydrates.

French Dressing

1/2 cup sugar
2/3 cup catsup
1/4 cup vinegar
1/3 cup salad oil
1 teaspoon salt
1 small grated onion
1 juice of a lemon

Put in a jar and shake well or put in blender.

This recipe came from Dad's Aunt Edith (married to Uncle Bill) who was the head chef at the Ace for many years.

Yield: 1 3/4 cups
Per Serving (excluding unknown items):
1246 Calories; 73g Fat (50.8% calories from fat);
4g Protein; 157g Carbohydrate; 4g Dietary Fiber;
0mg Cholesterol; 4034mg Sodium. Exchanges:
1-1/2 Vegetable; 14-1/2 Fat; 10 Other Carbohydrates.

Roma
Ranch Dressing Mix

1 cup parsley flakes
1/2 cup (15) crushed saltines
1/2 cup minced onions
1/2 cup garlic salt
1/2 cup onion salt
1/4 cup garlic powder
1/4 cup onion powder
2 tablespoons dill weed

Put in a jar and shake well or put in
blender.

Naomi
Mayonnaise

1 egg
3/4 teaspoon salt
1/2 teaspoon dry mustard
1 tablespoon vinegar
1 tablespoon lemon juice
1/4 teaspoon paprika
1/4 cup salad oil

Put all of the ingredients in a blender. Mix at
high speed then add another 3/4 cup oil
gradually while beating. (If it curdles, put 1/4
cup of the mixture and, with an additional
egg, beat, then add remaining mixture.)
Per Serving (excluding unknown items):
558 Calories; 59g Fat (93.6% calories from fat);
6g Protein; 3g Carbohydrate; Trace Dietary Fiber;
187mg Cholesterol; 1655mg Sodium. Exchanges:
0 Grain (Starch); 1 Lean Meat; 0 Fruit; 11-1/2 Fat;
0 Other Carbohydrates.

Soups

_____

_____

_____

_____

_____

_____

_____

Naomi
Chicken Dumpling Soup

4 cups chicken broth
flour
1 egg
1 dash salt and pepper, to taste

Beat egg. Put as much flour as the egg will hold. Add salt and pepper. Roll into small balls and put into boiling broth. Add pieces of chicken and carrots, onions, celery and spices to taste.

Per Serving (excluding unknown items):
219 Calories; 10g Fat (43.2% calories from fat);
25g Protein; 4g Carbohydrate; Trace Dietary Fiber;
187mg Cholesterol; 3286mg Sodium. Exchanges:
0 Grain (Starch); 2-1/2 Lean Meat; 1/2 Fat.

Naomi
Wild Rice soup

1-1/2 cups cooked wild rice
1/4 cup onion, chopped
6 tablespoons butter
6 tablespoons flour
1/4 teaspoon salt
1/8 teaspoon pepper
1 dash allspice
13-1/2 ounces chicken broth
1 cup half and half

Mix, heat and serve.
Yield: 6 cups
Per Serving (excluding unknown items):
277 Calories; 18g Fat (58.2% calories from fat);
6g Protein; 23g Carbohydrate; 2g Dietary Fiber; 47mg
Cholesterol; 616mg Sodium. Exchanges:
1-1/2 Grain (Starch); 0 Lean Meat; 0 Vegetable;
3-1/2 Fat.

Roma
Lentil and Bacon Soup

1 16oz bag dry lentils
32 ounces chicken broth
4 slices bacon
1 medium chopped onion
2 medium carrots, 1/4" slices
2 medium stalks celery, sliced
garlic
1 teaspoon salt
1/4 teaspoon pepper
1/4 teaspoon thyme

In covered 4-quart pan, heat lentils and broth
plus 4 cups water to boiling. Simmer 15
minutes. Cook and drain bacon. Use 1 tbs
bacon fat to sauté onions, carrots and celery.
Cook 5 min. Add garlic and cook for an
additional minute. Crumble bacon and add
salt, pepper, thyme and sautéed vegetables.
Cover and cook 5 mins more.
Per Serving (excluding unknown items):
410 Calories; 18g Fat (40.3% calories from fat);
29g Protein; 31g Carbohydrate; 8g Dietary Fiber; 22mg
Cholesterol; 5544mg Sodium. Exchanges:
0 Grain (Starch); 3 Lean Meat; 5 Vegetable; 2 Fat.

Roma
Hamburger Soup
from Marie Hoffmann

1-pound ground beef
1/4 teaspoon pepper
1/4 teaspoon oregano
1/4 teaspoon basil
1/4 teaspoon seasoned salt
1 package dry onion soup mix
4 cups boiling water
1 can 8oz can tomato sauce
1/4 cup parmesan cheese
1 tablespoon soy sauce
1 cup celery, sliced
1 cup carrots, sliced
1 cup shell pasta, cooked and drained

Brown ground beef, pepper, basil, oregano,
seasoned salt and dry soup mix. Put in crockpot.
Add water, tomato sauce, soy sauce, celery and
carrots. Cover and cook on low 6-8 hrs or on high
for 5 hrs. Add pasta and cheese, simmer another
15 minutes.
Per Serving (excluding unknown items):
643 Calories; 9g Fat (11.7% calories from fat);
28g Protein; 117g Carbohydrate; 12g Dietary Fiber;
16mg Cholesterol; 3411mg Sodium. Exchanges:
5-1/2 Grain (Starch); 1 Lean Meat; 6-1/2 vegetable;
1/2 Fat.

Roma
Chili
I always add cocoa to tomato based casseroles.

1-pound ground or chipped beef
1 large can stewed tomatoes
1 15oz can tomato sauce
3 tablespoons brown sugar
2 tablespoons molasses
1 medium onion, chopped
8 ounces mushrooms, canned or fresh
4 ounces mozzarella cheese
1 tablespoon worcestershire sauce
1 teaspoon salt
1/2 teaspoon cocoa powder
1/4 teaspoon coarse ground pepper
sour cream to suit

Brown the beef and onion. Add the rest of the ingredients, except sour cream and simmer for at least an hour. Serve with a dollop of sour cream and crackers.
Yield: 6 servings
Per Serving (excluding unknown items):
126 Calories; 5g Fat (33.6% calories from fat);
6g Protein; 16g Carbohydrate; 1g Dietary Fiber; 17mg Cholesterol; 476mg Sodium. Exchanges:
0 Grain (Starch); 1/2 Lean Meat; 1 Vegetable;
1/2 Fat; 1/2 Other

Roma
Microwave Freezing Corn

6 ears com, husked and cleaned

Place corn in a 12" x 8" dish. Cover. Use NO
water. Cook 5-1/2 minutes on high. Turn once
midway. Let stand 1 minute. Chill in ice water.
Package and freeze.
Yield: 6 servings
Per Serving (excluding unknown items):
77 Calories; 1g Fat (10.7% Calories from fat);
3g Protein; 17g Carbohydrate; 2g Dietary Fiber;
0mg Cholesterol; 14rng Sodium. Exchanges:
1 Grain (Starch).

Meats

_____

_____

_____

_____

_____

_____

_____

_____

_____

Naomi
Roast or Meat Loaf Flavoring

2 tablespoons vinegar
2 tablespoons molasses
1 tablespoon sugar
1 smidgen minced onion
1 dash cloves, allspice, pepper and salt

Mix together.
Per Serving (excluding unknown items):
203 Calories; Trace Fat (0.9% calories from fat);
1g Protein; 52g Carbohydrate; 2g Dietary Fiber; 0mg
Cholesterol; 19mg Sodium. Exchanges:
1/2 Vegetable; 3 Other Carbohydrates.

Mildred
Tavern Burgers
Just like sloppy joes

1 medium onion
3/4 cup water
1 teaspoon salt.
1 teaspoon horseradish
1 teaspoon mustard
1/3 cup catsup
1/2 teaspoon pepper
1/2 teaspoon chili powder
1 tablespoon sugar
1-pound ground beef

Combine all but beef and bring to a boil, add
beef and simmer. Serve on fresh buns.
per Serving (excluding unknown items):
1593 Calories; 121g Fat (68.7% calories from fat); 78g
Protein; 46g Carbohydrate; 4g Dietary Fiber; 386mg
Cholesterol; 3479mg Sodium. Exchanges:
0 Grain (Starch); 11 Lean Meat; 1-1/2 Vegetable; 18
Fat; 2-1/2 Other Carbohydrates.

Naomi
Mince Meat
From Aunt Belle

1 pound rather fat beef, boiled and ground
5 apples, cut up
1 cup raisins
1 cup currants
1 cup brown sugar
1 teaspoon cloves
vinegar to taste
water from boiling to moisten

Cook until apples are done.
Yield: 1 pie
Per Serving (excluding unknown items):
228 Calories; 1g Fat (2.0% calories from fat);
1g Protein; 59g Carbohydrate; 5g Dietary Fiber; 0mg
Cholesterol; 12mg Sodium. Exchanges:
0 Grain (Starch): 2-1/2 Fruit; 0 Fat; 1-1/2 Other
Carbohydrates.

Roma
**Kohl Dolmer-Cabbage
Rolls**
Remember?

12 cabbage leaves
1-pound ground beef
1/2 cup instant rice, uncooked
1 can tomato sauce, 15 oz
1/2 teaspoon salt
1 dash pepper
1 medium onion, chopped
1 clove garlic, finely chopped
1 teaspoon sugar
1/2 teaspoon lemon juice
1 tablespoon cornstarch
1 tablespoon water

Cover cabbage leaves with boiling water.
Cover and let stand about 10 min. Drain.
Mix beef, rice, salt, pepper, onion and garlic.
Place about 1/3 cup of beef mixture in each
cabbage leaf. (Remove thick stems). Place
rolls, seam side down, in ungreased baking
dish. Mix tomato sauce, sugar and lemon
juice. Pour over rolls.
Cover and bake at 350° for 45 min.
Remove cabbage rolls to plate. Mix
cornstarch and water. Stir liquid in pan.
Heat to boiling and boil 1 min. Pour over rolls
and serve

Yield: 12 rolls

Per Serving (excluding unknown items):
411 Calories; 30g Fat (66.4% calories from fat);
21g Protein; 14g Carbohydrate: 3g Dietary Fiber; 96mg
Cholesterol; 728mg Sodium. Exchanges:
0 Grain (Starch): 2-1/2 Lean Meat; 2 Vegetable;
0 Fruit; 4-1/2 Fat; 0 Other Carbohydrates.

Roma
Mock Chicken Legs
Dad's specialty
1/2 a pound beef, cubed
1/2 a pound pork, cubed
1/2 a pound veal, cubed
1 dash pepper
1 teaspoon salt
1 egg
cracker crumbs
Ask your butcher for skewer sticks (if that's
still where you can get them). Alternate the
three meats onto sticks. Salt and pepper
them. Dip into beaten egg and cracker
crumbs. Sauté in small amount of oil until no
longer pink inside. Serving Ideas: Dad makes
these when he's
compelled to cook. Suzy calls them
"schmocks".
Yield: 4 servings
Per Serving (excluding unknown items):
370 Calories; 25g Fat (63.1% calories from fat);
33g Protein; Trace Carbohydrate; Trace Dietary Fiber;
170mg Cholesterol; 656mg Sodium. Exchanges: 0
Grain (Starch); 4-1/2 Lean Meat:
2-1/2 Fat.

Naomi
B B Que Sauce

1 bottle Open Pit style barbeque sauce
1 bottle Open Pit style barbeque sauce with
onions
1 cup grape jelly

Heat until blended and pour over meat.
Per Serving (excluding unknown items):
824 Calories; Trace Fat (0.2% calories from fat);
1g Protein; 215g Carbohydrate; 3g Dietary Fiber; 0mg
Cholesterol; 109mg Sodium. Exchanges:
14 Other Carbohydrates.

Naomi
Spaghetti Sauce

1 medium onion, chopped
1-pound ground sirloin
2 small cans tomato sauce
2 cans tomato paste
1/2 cup red wine
1/2 cup water
1 teaspoon salt
2 tablespoons olive oil
1 clove garlic, minced
1/2 teaspoon sugar
1 teaspoon oregano
1/2 teaspoon pepper

Brown beef and onion until redness disappears. Add remaining ingredients and simmer 1-1/2 hrs.

Per Serving (excluding unknown items):
1809 Calories; 107g Fat (54.0% calories from fat);
103g Protein; 102g Carbohydrate; 21g Dietary Fiber;
313mg Cholesterol; 7550mg Sodium.
Exchanges 0 Grain (Starch); 12-1/2 Lean Meat;
17-1/2 Vegetable; 13-1/2 Fat; 0 Other Carbohydrates.

Roma
Blender Hollandaise
In case you don't have a mix.

3 egg yolks
2 tablespoons lemon juice
1 dash cayenne pepper
1/2 cup butter, melted
1 dash salt, to taste

Combine egg yolks, lemon juice, and
cayenne in blender at high speed. Add hot
melted butter in a steady stream,
Per Serving (excluding unknown items):
1000 Calories; 107g Fat (94.8% calories from fat); 9g
Protein; 4g Carbohydrate; Trace Dietary Fiber; 886mg
Cholesterol; 1225rng Sodium. Exchanges: 0 Grain
(Starch); 1 Lean Meat; 0 Fruit; 20-1/2 Fat.

Roma
Jerky

1-1/2 pounds meat, venison or beef
1/4 cup soy sauce
1/4 cup worcestershire sauce
1 teaspoon liquid smoke flavoring
1/2 teaspoon garlic powder
1 teaspoon onion powder
1 teaspoon MSG, optional
1/3 teaspoon fresh ground pepper
1/3 teaspoon salt

Cut meat into strips. Mix remaining ingredients and marinate meat strips in mixture for 24 hrs. Lay strips on oven racks (shelves) and bake at the oven's lowest temperature for at least 8 hrs until dry.
Per Serving (excluding unknown items):
102 Calories; Trace Fat (1.4% calories from fat);
6g Protein; 20g Carbohydrate; 1g Dietary Fiber; Trace Cholesterol; 6032mg Sodium. Exchanges:
0 Grain (Starch); 0 Lean Meat; 1-1/2 Vegetable;
0 Fat; 1/2 Other Carbohydrates.

Casseroles and Hotdishes

Naomi
Ham Casserole

1 cup cooked ham, cubed
4 ounces noodles
1/2 cup Velveeta style American cheese, cut
in pieces
1/2 cup milk
1/2 can mushroom soup
1 dash pepper

Cook noodles in salted water. Mix with other
ingredients and bake in buttered casserole
dish with crushed potato chips on top. Bake
45 minutes at 350^0

Per Serving (excluding unknown items):
818 Calories; 28g Fat (30.7% calories from fat);
45g Protein; 95g Carbohydrate: 3g Dietary Fiber;
202mg Cholesterol; 2302mg Sodium. Exchanges:
5-1/2 Grain (Starch); 3-1/2 Lean Meat; 1/2 Non-Fat
Milk; 3-1/2 Fat.

Roma
Tuna Casserole
Remember lunch?

8 ounces potato chips, crushed
1 can water-packed tuna, drained
1 can mushroom soup
1/2 cup milk
1/4 cup cheddar cheese, shredded
1/4 teaspoon dry mustard

Place 1/2 the crushed chips in a 10" baking dish. Arrange tuna over chips. Cover with remaining chips. Combine soup and milk and pour over all. Sprinkle with cheese and bake at 325^0 for 20-25 min. Remove from oven and let stand for 5 min. Serve.
Yield: 4 servings
Per Serving (excluding unknown items):
384 Calories; 25g Fat (58.1% calories from fat);
7g Protein; 34g Carbohydrate; 3g Dietary Fiber; 12mg Cholesterol; 616mg Sodium. Exchanges:
2 Grain (Starch); 1/2 Lean Meat; 0 Non-Fat Milk;
5 Fat.

Roma
Chow Mein Casserole

1 cup rice
3-1/2 cups water, boiling
1 teaspoon salt
2 tablespoons brown sugar
2 tablespoons soy sauce
1-pound hamburger
1 small onion, minced
2 cups celery, diced
1 can mushroom soup

Put first 5 ingredients in baking dish. Brown hamburger with onion and add to dish. Add celery and soup. Bake covered for 1/2 hour and uncovered for another 1/2 hour (350^0)
Yield: 6 servings
Per Serving (excluding unknown items):
393 Calories; 12g Fat (26.8% calories from fat);
14g Protein; 58g Carbohydrate; 2g Dietary Fiber; 30mg Cholesterol; 1213mg Sodium. Exchanges:
3-1/2 Grain (Starch); 1 Lean Meat; 1/2 vegetable:
2 Fat; 0 Other Carbohydrates.

Roma
One-Pot Bean Dinner
From Suzy

1-pound ground beef
3/4-pound bacon
1 cup onion, chopped
3 cans pork and beans, 31 oz cans
1 can kidney beans, 16 oz can, drained
1 cup catsup
1 can butter beans, 16 oz can
1/4 cup brown sugar
1 tablespoon liquid smoke flavoring
3 tablespoons vinegar
1 teaspoon salt
Brown hamburger, drain off fat and put beef
in crock pot. Brown bacon and onions, drain.
Add bacon, onions and remaining ingredients
to crock pot. Stir. Cook 4-9 hours on low.

Yield: 1 casserole
Per Serving (excluding unknown items):
843 Calories; 49g Fat (51.8% calories from fat);
45g Protein; 57g Carbohydrate; 17g Dietary Fiber;
113mg Cholesterol; 1829mg Sodium. Exchanges:
2-1/2 Grain (Starch); 5 Lean Meat; 1/2 Vegetable;
7 Fat; 1 Other Carbohydrates.

Naomi
Impossible Lasagna Pie
From Mary Ackerknecht

1/2 cup small curd cottage cheese
1/4 cup parmesan cheese
1-pound ground beef, cooked and drained
1 teaspoon dried oregano leaves
1/2 teaspoon basil leaves
1 can tomato paste
1 cup mozzarella cheese, shredded
1 cup milk
2/3 cup Bisquick@ baking mix
2 eggs
1 teaspoon salt
1/4 teaspoon pepper

Lightly grease 10" pie plate and layer cottage cheese and parmesan cheese in plate. Mix beef, oregano, basil, tomato paste and 1/2 cup of mozzarella cheese. Spoon evenly over the top. Beat milk, Bisquick, eggs, salt and pepper until smooth. Pour into plate. Bake 30-35 min at 400⁰. Sprinkle with remaining cheese. Let stand 5 min before cutting.
Yield: 1 pie
Per Serving (excluding unknown items):
428 Calories; 30g Fat.

Naomi
Lasagna

1/2-pound (about 12 strips) lasagna noodles
16 oz ricotta cheese (2-1/2 cups)
2 eggs
3/4 cup parmesan cheese
2 tablespoons parsley flakes
1-pound mozzarella cheese, shredded
Spaghetti sauce - recipe or canned

Cook noodles per box directions. Drain and rinse.
Beat eggs, add ricotta, 1/2 cup parmesan,
parsley, salt and pepper to taste.
Layer half the noodles in a 13 x 9 x 2 baking dish.
Spread with half of the ricotta filling. Add half of
the meat sauce. Repeat layers. Sprinkle
remaining parmesan on top. Bake at 375^0 for 30-
35 minutes. Let stand 10 minutes.

Sunday Night Supper

Make thin pancakes from your favorite recipe or mix. Fill them with a mixture of browned ground beef, onions and seasonings. Add a slightly beaten egg and sour cream or cottage cheese. Roll up and bake about 15 minutes. Serve with tomato sauce seasoned with salt and pepper and sprinkle with parmesan.
Per Serving (excluding unknown items):
0 Calories; 0g Fat (0.0% calories from fat);
0g Protein; 0g Carbohydrate; 0g Dietary Fiber;
0rng Cholesterol; 0rng Sodium.

Roma
Corn Pudding

2 cups corn, fresh or canned
1 teaspoon sugar
1 teaspoon salt
1/4 teaspoon pepper
2 eggs, well-beaten
1 cup milk
1 tablespoon butter
2 tablespoons cracker crumbs

Heat oven to 350^0. Mix ingredients. Pour into buttered 1 qt baking dish. Set in pan of hot water l" deep. Bake 60-70 min.

Yield: 1 casserole
Per Serving (excluding unknown items):
111 Calories; 5g Fat (40.7% calories from fat);
5g Protein; 13g Carbohydrate; 1g Dietary Fiber; 73mg Cholesterol: 421mg Sodium. Exchanges:
1/2 Grain (Starch); 1/2 Lean Meat; 0 Non-Fat Milk; 1 Fat; O Other Carbohydrates.

Naomi
Kluski
Grandpa's favorite.

5 med size potatoes
1 egg
1 dash salt and pepper
flour

Cook and mash potatoes. Cool. Mix in egg.
Add as much flour as it will take. This varies
with the moistness of the potatoes. Form into
dumpling size pieces and drop in boiling
water. Serving Ideas: Serve with gravy or
meat juices, preferably pork.

Per Serving (excluding unknown items):
548 Calories; 5g Fat (8.1 % calories from fat);
18g Protein; 110g Carbohydrate; 10g Dietary
Fiber; 187mg Cholesterol; 270mg Sodium. Exchanges:
7-1/2 Grain (starch); 1 Lean Meat;
1/2 Fat.

Cakes and Frostings

_____

_____

_____

_____

_____

_____

_____

_____

Naomi
Date Nut Cake
Recipe from Aunt Belle. I have no idea about temperature and time.

1 cup sugar
2 tablespoons lard
2 large eggs
1/2 teaspoon salt
1 teaspoon vanilla
1 pound of dates
1/2 cup nuts, chopped
1 teaspoon soda
1 cup boiling water
1-1/3 cups flour

Mix together sugar, lard, eggs, salt and vanilla. Set aside. Pour the boiling water over the dates, nuts and soda and let stand. Mix all together and add flour. Bake
Yield: 12 servings
Per Serving (excluding unknown items):
276 Calories; 6g Fat (20.1 % calories from fat);
4g Protein; 54g Carbohydrate; 4g Dietary Fiber; 33mg Cholesterol; 101 mg

Naomi
Cold Water Fruit Cake
Aunt Belle's Recipe

1 cup shortening
2 cups sugar
1 pound of walnuts
3 cups flour
1 cup cold water
1 large tsp soda
1 pound of seeded raisins
4 eggs
1 teaspoon each of cloves, cinnamon,
nutmeg, salt.

Mix and bake
Yield: 20 servings
Per Serving (excluding unknown items):
454 Calories; 24g Fat (46.0% calories from fat);
9g Protein; 55g Carbohydrate; 3g Dietary Fiber; 37mg
Cholesterol; 19mg Sodium. Exchanges:
1 Grain (Starch); 1 Lean Meat; 1 Fruit; 4-1/2 Fat;
1-1/2 Other Carbohydrates.

Naomi
Orange Cupcakes
Copied from grandma 's notes.

1 cup sugar
1/3 cup shortening
1 cup raisins
1 cup buttermilk
 medium orange, ground fine
2 scant cups flour
1 teaspoon soda
1 teaspoon baking powder
1 pinch salt

That's all!!
Yield: 12 servings
Per Serving (excluding unknown items):
241 Calories; 6g Fat (22.4% calories from fat);
3g Protein; 44g Carbohydrate; 1g Dietary Fiber;
1mg Cholesterol; 75mg Sodium. Exchanges:
1 Grain (Starch); 1/2 Fruit; 0 Non-Fat Milk; 1 Fat;
1 Other Carbohydrates.

Naomi
Children's Spongecake
We had this often.

2 eggs
milk
2 teaspoons baking powder
1-1/2 cups flour
1 cup sugar
1 pinch salt
flavoring

Break the eggs in a cup and fill with milk or
cream. Add the rest of the ingredients.
Yield: 12 servings
Per Serving (excluding unknown items):
133 Calories; 1g Fat (6.0% calories from fat);
3g Protein; 29g Carbohydrate; Trace Dietary Fiber;
31mg Cholesterol; 102mg Sodium. Exchanges:
1 Grain (Starch); 0 Lean Meat; 0 Fat;
1 Other Carbohydrates.

Roma
Chilled Triple Chocolate Cake

1 package fudge cake mix
1 package chocolate frosting mix
1/3 cup chocolate ice cream topping

Prepare cake mix as directed on package. Pour batter into two 8" or 9" layer pans, greased and floured. Bake as directed on pkg. Cool layers 15 minutes before removing from pans. Cool completely. Prepare frosting as directed on package. Spread half of frosting between cooled layers; spread remaining half on top. Drizzle the chocolate topping over top of entire cake. Refrigerate until ready to serve.

Yield: 1 layer cake

Per Serving (excluding unknown. items): 4 Calories; Trace Fat (11,1% calories from fat); Trace Protein; 1g Carbohydrate; Trace Dietary Fiber;
0mg Cholesterol; 1mg Sodium. Exchanges: 0 Fat;
0 Other Carbohydrates.

Naomi
Spice Cake
Written by Grandma

1 cup raisins
1 cup raisin juice, cooled
1/3 cup shortening
1 cup sugar
1 egg, or none
2 cups flour (about)
Baking powder, salt, spices, nuts etc.

Boil raisins 20 min. Mix and bake.
Yield: 15 servings
Per Serving (excluding unknown items):
186 Calories; 5g Fat (24.0% calories from fat);
2g Protein; 34g Carbohydrate; 1g Dietary Fiber; 12mg
Cholesterol; 5mg Sodium. Exchanges:
1 Grain (Starch); 0 Lean Meat; 1/2 Fruit; 1 Fat;
1 Other Carbohydrates.

Roma
Delectable Dumpcake

1 can (15oz) crushed pineapple
1 can (15oz) cherry pie filling
1 package yellow or white cake mix
1/2 cup butter, cold
1 cup nuts, chopped

Put pineapple (undrained) and pie filling into a
13" x 9" ungreased cake pan. Mix together
well. Spread the dry cake mix over this
mixture. Slice very thin and lay pats of butter
over the cake mix. (One stick of butter should
cover the entire cake.) Sprinkle chopped nuts
over the top of the butter. There is no mixing
necessary. Bake at 400^0 for 1 hour. (The
cake may smell or look like it is over baking,
but it isn't.)

Yield: 1 cake
Per Serving (excluding unknown items):
121 Calories; 9g Fat (61.4% calories from fat);
1g Protein; 11g Carbohydrate; 1g Dietary Fiber; 12mg
Cholesterol; 50mg Sodium. Exchanges:
0 Grain (Starch); 0 Lean Meat; 0 Fruit, 1-1/2 Fat; 1/2
Other Carbohydrates.

Roma
Carrot Cake

1 box yellow cake mix
1-1/4 cups Miracle Whip Salad Dressing
4 eggs
1/4 cup cold water
2 teaspoons cinnamon
2 cups carrots, finely shredded
1/2 cup walnuts, chopped

Combine cake mix, salad dressing, eggs, water and cinnamon, mixing at med speed until well blended. Stir in carrots and walnuts. Pour into greased 13" x 9" baking pan. Bake at 350^0 for 35 min or until toothpick comes out clean. Cool and frost with vanilla or caramel frosting.

Yield: 1 cake
Per Serving (excluding unknown items):
150 Calories; 6g Fat (33.5% calories from fat);
3g Protein; 22g Carbohydrate; 1g Dietary Fiber; 38mg Cholesterol; 186mg Sodium. Exchanges:
0 Grain (Starch); 1/2 Lean Meat; 1/2 Vegetable;
1 Fat; 1-1/2 Other Carbohydrates.

Mildred
Black Midnight Devil's Food Cake

1/2 cup shortening
1-1/4 cups sugar
2 large eggs
1/2 cup hot coffee
1/2 cup cocoa powder
1-1/2 cups flour
1/2 teaspoon salt
1 teaspoon soda
1/4 teaspoon baking powder

Combine cocoa and hot coffee. Add to creamed shortening, sugar and eggs alternately with dry ingredients that have been sifted together. Bake in greased square cake pan (9") at 350^0 for 45-55 min. Serving Ideas: Hard as I have tried, I can never make this as good as Grandma Mildred did.

Yield: I cake
Per Serving (excluding unknown items):
232 Calories; 10g Fat (37.0% calories from fat); 3g Protein; 35g Carbohydrate; 2g Dietary Fiber; 31mg Cholesterol; 110mg Sodium. Exchanges: 1 Grain (Starch); 0 Lean Meat; 2 Fat; 1-1/2 Other Carbohydrates.

Naomi
Decorating Icing

1/4 cup shortening (can be part butter)
4 cups powdered sugar
2 tablespoons cream
1 egg white
1-1/2 teaspoons vanilla

Blend all ingredients on low speed and beat
on high until fluffy.
Yield: 2 cups
Per Serving (excluding unknown items):
1975 Calories; 8g Fat (3.6% calories from fat);
4g Protein; 481g Carbohydrate; 0g Dietary Fiber; 26mg
Cholesterol; 71mg Sodium. Exchanges:
1/2 Lean Meat; 1-1/2 Fat; 32 Other Carbohydrates.

Naomi
Rhubarb Cake

1/2 cup shortening
2 cups flour
1 cup sugar
1 egg
1 cup sour milk
2-1/2 cups rhubarb
1 teaspoon soda
1/2 teaspoon cinnamon
Mix and bake at 350^0 for 40 min.
Yield: 1 cake
Per Serving (excluding unknown items):
2659 Calories; 109g Fat (36.8% calories from fat); 31g
Protein; 392g Carbohydrate; 8g Dietary Fiber; 187mg
Cholesterol; 63mg Sodium. Exchanges:
12-1/2 Grain (Starch); 1 Lean Meat; 21 Fat;
13-1/2 Other Carbohydrates.

Roma
Angel Food Cake

Prepare-let eggs stand at room temperature, an hour or 2 before using. Use ungreased 10" tube pan.

1 cup + 2 tablespoons sifted cake flour
1/2 cups sifted granulated sugar
1-1/4 cups egg whites
1/4 teaspoon salt
1-1/4 teaspoons cream of tartar
1 cup sifted sugar
1 teaspoon vanilla
1/4 teaspoon almond extract
Sift flour with 1/2 cup of sugar - 4 times
Beat egg whites and salt with wire whisk until foamy. Sprinkle in cream of tartar and beat until eggs are stiff enough to hold up in soft peaks. Add remaining 1 cup sugar in 4 additions by sprinkling 4 tablespoons at a time over egg whites, add flavoring and beat. Add flour and sugar in 4 additions, sifting it over the egg whites, fold in. Bake in moderate oven 375° 30 - 35 minutes.

Roma
Zucchini Cake
Beat until fluffy:

3 eggs

2 cups sugar

2 teaspoons vanilla

1 cup oil

Add:

2 cups grated zucchini

Sift and add:

3 cups flour

1 teaspoon baking powder

1 teaspoon salt

1 teaspoon soda

Add:

1 cup crushed pineapple

1/2 cup raisins

1 cup chopped pecans

To egg and sugar mixture, add zucchini, then flour mixture. Stir in pineapple, raisins and pecans. Mix well. Bake in large sheet cake pan. 10 x 14 well-greased and floured at 325^0 for 1 hour.

Frosting:

3 ozs softened cream cheese

2 cups powdered sugar

1 stick margarine

1 teaspoon vanilla

Naomi
White Frosting
From Eileen

2 egg whites, beaten 'til stiff
1/2 cup butter
1/2 cup lard
1 cup sugar, extra fine
1/3 cup milk
1 dash vanilla

Beat egg whites until stiff, set aside.
Cream butter, lard and sugar. Add egg
whites and beat. Bring milk to a hard boil
and add to mixture. Add vanilla and beat.
Yield: 1 cake
Per Serving (excluding unknown items):
1672 Calories; 95g Fat (49.8% calories from fat); 11g
Protein; 204g Carbohydrate; 0g Dietary Fiber; 259mg
Cholesterol; 1088mg Sodium. Exchanges:
1 Lean Meat; 1/2 Non-Fat Milk; 19 Fat; 13-1/2 Other
carbohydrates.

Naomi
Chocolate Frosting
From Mrs. Kalkman

1 cup sugar
2 squares chocolate, cut up
1 egg
2 Tablespoons butter
3 Tablespoons milk

Bring to boil. Remove from fire. Add dash of vanilla and beat.

Yield: 1 cake covering
Per Serving (excluding unknown items):
1357 Calories; 48g Fat (30.7% calories from fat);
9g Protein; 236g Carbohydrate; 3g Dietary Fiber;
255mg Cholesterol; 323mg Sodium. Exchanges:
1 Lean Meat; 0 Non-Fat Milk; 9 Fat; 15-1/2 Other
Carbohydrates.

Naomi
Carmel Frosting
From Aunt Phil

1 cup brown sugar
1/3 cup shortening
1/4 cup milk
1 cup powdered sugar

Boil all ingredients for 3 min and cool.
Beat in powdered sugar.
Yield: I cake covering
Per Serving (excluding unknown items):
1654 Calories; 70g Fat (37.4% calories from fat);
2g Protein; 263g Carbohydrate; 0g Dietary Fiber; 8mg
Cholesterol; 88mg Sodium. Exchanges:
0 Non-Fat Milk; 14 Fat; 17-1/2 Other Carbohydrates.

Roma
Decorating Icing

1/4 cup shortening (can be part butter)
4 cups powdered sugar
2 tablespoons cream
1 egg white
1-1/2 teaspoons vanilla

Blend all ingredients on low speed and beat
on high until fluffy.
Yield: 2 cups
Per Serving (excluding unknown items):
1975 Calories; 8g Fat (3.6% calories from fat);
4g Protein; 481g Carbohydrate; 0g Dietary Fiber; 26mg
Cholesterol; 71mg Sodium. Exchanges:
1/2 Lean Meat; 1-1/2 Fat; 32 Other Carbohydrates.

Roma
Rocky Road Frosting

3 squares unsweetened chocolate
1/4 cup butter
1 egg
1/4 teaspoon salt
1 lb. powdered sugar
2-3 tablespoons hot water
1/2 cup nuts
1/2 cup miniature marshmallows

Melt chocolate and butter over boiling water.
Beat egg and salt, gradually add chocolate
mixture, beating well. Gradually add
powdered sugar alternating with hot water.
Add nuts and marshmallows.

Pies

_____

_____

_____

_____

_____

_____

_____

_____

Naomi
Rhubarb No-Crust Pie

4 cups cut up rhubarb
3/4 cup sugar
2 tablespoons butter
1 cup flour
1 cup sugar
2 eggs, beaten
1 teaspoon vanilla
1 tablespoon lemon juice

Grease a 9" or 10" pie tin. Sprinkle with a little flour. Spoon rhubarb into pie tin and sprinkle 3/4 c sugar over all. Cut butter into the cup of flour as for pie crust. Add the cup of sugar and mix well. Stir eggs into the butter/flour mixture. Batter will be very stiff. Spoon on top of rhubarb as evenly as possible. Sprinkle lemon juice on top. Bake at 325^0 for 1 hour.

Yield: 1 pie
Per Serving (excluding unknown items):
360 Calories; 6g Fat (13.6% calories from fat);
4g Protein; 75g

Naomi
Pie Crust
It's the lard!!

1-1/4 cups flour
1/3 cup lard
4 tablespoons cold water
1 pinch salt

Mix cold lard into flour until it forms pea-size pieces. Mix in cold (preferably ice) water and salt until it makes a dough that is easy to handle. Roll until it will fit a 9" pie pan. Prick with a fork over bottom of crust and bake at 475^0 for 8 to 10 min, or fill with pie filling and cover with a second crust. Use an egg wash or milk or sprinkle with sugar,
Yield: I crust
Per Serving (excluding unknown items):
1184 Calories; 70g Fat (53.7% calories from fat);
16g protein; 119g Carbohydrate; 5g Dietary Fiber;
65mg Cholesterol; 138mg Sodium. Exchanges:
8 Grain (Starch); 13-1/2 Fat.

Mildred
Pecan Pie

1/4 cup butter
1/2 cup sugar
3/4 cup dark syrup
3 eggs, slightly beaten
1 teaspoon vanilla
1 cup pecans, chopped or halved

Cream together butter and sugar. Add
syrup, eggs, vanilla and pecans. Pour into
pie crust. Bake at 350^0 for 55 min.

Serving Ideas: Serve with whipped cream
or ice cream.
Yield: 1 pie
Per Serving (excluding unknown items):
287 Calories; 22g Fat (66.8% calories from fat);
4g Protein; 20g Carbohydrate; 1g Dietary Fiber; 114mg
Cholesterol; 106mg Sodium. Exchanges:
0 Grain (Starch); 1/2 Lean Meat; 4 Fat;
1 Other Carbohydrates.

Naomi
Lemon Pie
From Aunt Phil

1/3 cup oleo, melted
1/3 cup lemon juice
1 1/2 teaspoons unflavored gelatin
2 eggs, separated
3 Tablespoons sugar
1 can sweetened condensed milk
1 graham cracker crust

In a small sauce pan combine lemon juice
and gelatin, heat until gelatin melts. Cool. In a
mixing bowl, beat egg
whites and add sugar. Beat egg yolks, add
milk and gelatin mixture. Fold in egg whites.
Pour into crust and chill 2 hrs.
Sprinkle crumbs over top.
Yield: 1 pie
Per Serving (excluding unknown items):
214 Calories; 6g Fat (24.4% calories from fat);
6g Protein; 35g Carbohydrate; 0g Dietary Fiber: 80mg
Cholesterol; 86mg Sodium. Exchanges:
1/2 Lean Meat; 1 Fat; 2-1/2 Other Carbohydrates.

Naomi
Nutcracker Pie
Servings: 12
Great and Easy

3 egg whites
1 cup sugar
12 soda crackers, crushed
1 teaspoon baking powder
1 teaspoon vanilla
3/4 cup nuts, chopped

Beat egg whites until stiff, gradually beat in sugar, add crackers, baking powder, vanilla and nuts. Put into pie pan and bake at 350^0 for 30 min. Serving Ideas: Serve with whipped cream and crushed pineapple or berries

Yield: 20 squares
Per Serving (excluding unknown items):
125 Calories: 5g Fat (34.7% calories from fat);
2g Protein; 19g Carbohydrate; 1g Dietary Fiber; 0mg Cholesterol; 55mg Sodium. Exchanges:
0 Grain (Starch); 1/2 Lean Meat; 1 Fat; 1 Other Carbohydrates.

Roma
French Silk Chocolate Pie

1/2 cup butter
3/4 cup sugar
1 square baking chocolate, melted and
cooled
1 teaspoon vanilla
2 eggs

Cream together butter and sugar. Blend in
chocolate and vanilla. Beat in eggs, one at a
time, beating on medium speed of mixer five
minutes after each. Pour in prepared pie shell
and chill 1-2 hours.

Yield: 1 pie
Per Serving (excluding unknown items):
281 Calories; 19g Fat (59.9% calories from fat);
2g Protein; 27g Carbohydrate; 1g Dietary Fiber; 104mg
Cholesterol; 176mg Sodium. Exchanges:
0 Grain (Starch); 1/2 Lean Meat; 3 Fat;1/1/2 Other
Carbohydrates.

Roma
Mock Apple Pie
Tastes like real Apple Pie

1-1/2 cups sugar.
1-1/2 cups water
1-1/2 teaspoons cream of tartar
1 teaspoon cinnamon
1 dash nutmeg
1 teaspoon lemon juice
16 ritz crackers
2 9" pie crusts
1 dab butter

Combine the first five ingredients and boil 5 min. Cool. Add lemon juice. Place crackers in 1/4" thick pastry. Pour cooled syrup over crackers. Dot with butter. Cover with second piecrust. Use milk or egg wash and brush top of pie crust. Bake at 400^0 for 35 min. Serving Ideas: Serve warm with ice cream or cheese.
Yield: 1 pie
Per Serving (excluding unknown items):
332 Calories: 15g Fat (40.4% calories from fat); Trace Protein; 51g Carbohydrate; Trace Dietary Fiber; 41mg Cholesterol; 159mg Sodium. Exchanges:0 Grain (Starch); 0 Fruit; 3 Fat; 3-1/2 Other Carbohydrates.

Mildred
Angel Pie
DELICIOUS!

1 pie crust, pre-baked
1 cup sugar
2 tablespoons flour
2 tablespoons cornstarch
1/2 teaspoon salt
2 cups hot water
2 egg whites, beaten until stiff
1/2 teaspoon vanilla
1/2 teaspoon almond extract
1/2 cup maraschino cherries, chopped

Mix together sugar, flour, cornstarch and salt.
Add the hot water. Bring to a boil and boil for 12
min. Cool. Beat the egg whites until stiff and fold
into cool mixture. Add vanilla and almond extract.
Pour into baked pie shell. Let stand overnight.
Cover with whipped cream and top with chopped
cherries.
Yield: 1 Pie
Per Serving (excluding unknown items):
313 Calories; 8g Fat (23.2% calories from fat);
3g Protein; 58g Carbohydrate; 1g Dietary Fiber; 0mg
Cholesterol; 403mg Sodium. Exchanges:
1 Grain (Starch); 0 Lean Meat; 1-1/2 Fat;
 2-1/2 other

Roma
Lemon Meringue Pie

1 baked pie shell
1-1/4 cups sugar
6 tablespoons cornstarch
2 cups water
1/3 cup lemon juice
3 eggs, separated
3 tablespoons butter
1-1/2 teaspoons lemon extract
2 teaspoons vinegar

Mix sugar and cornstarch together in top of double boiler. Add water. Combine egg yolks with lemon juice and beat. Add to first mixture. Cook until thick (approx. 25 min). Add lemon extract, butter and vinegar, stir. Pour into shell, cool. Top with meringue. (Made with the remaining egg whites)
Yield: I pie
Per Serving (excluding unknown items):
280 Calories; 8g Fat (25.1% calories from fat):
3g Protein; 50g Carbohydrate; Trace Dietary Fiber;
109mg Cholesterol; 90mg Sodium. Exchanges:
1/2 Grain (Starch); 1/2 Lean Meat; 0 Fruit;
1-/2 Fat; 3 Other Carbohydrates.

Roma
Never-Fail Meringue

1 tablespoon cornstarch
2 tablespoons cold water
1/2 cup boiling water
3 egg whites
6 tablespoons sugar
1 teaspoon vanilla
1 pinch salt

Blend cornstarch and cold water in saucepan. Add boiling water and cook, stirring until clear and thick. Let stand until COLD. Gradually add sugar to beaten egg whites, beat until stiff. Add salt and vanilla. Gradually beat in cold cornstarch mixture. Turn mixer on high speed and beat well. Spread meringue on pie and bake at 350^0 for 10 min.

Yield: I pie
Per Serving (excluding unknown items):
64 Calories; Trace Fat (00% calories from fat);
2g Protein; 14g Carbohydrate; Trace Dietary Fiber;
0mg Cholesterol; 51mg Sodium. Exchanges:
0 Grain (Starch); 0 Lean Meat; 1 Other Carbohydrates.

Roma

Pumpkin Pie

2 unbaked pie shells
1 large of can pumpkin
6 eggs, slightly beaten
2 cups white or light brown sugar, or
some of each
1 teaspoon salt
2 teaspoons cinnamon
1/2 teaspoon cloves
1/2 teaspoon nutmeg
1/2 teaspoon ginger
2 cups evaporated milk

Prepare the two pie shells. Combine eggs, sugar, salt and spices and beat well. Blend in canned pumpkin. Add milk and beat well. Pour into pastry lined pans. Bake at 450^0 for 10 min, then reduce heat and bake 350^0 for 40-45 min.

Yield: 2 pies
Per Serving (excluding unknown items):
70 Calories; 4g Fat (52.1% calories from fat);
4g Protein; 4g Carbohydrate; Trace Dietary Fiber:
79mg Cholesterol; 188mg Sodium. Exchanges:
0 Grain (Starch); 1/2 Lean Meat; 1/2 Non-Fat Milk; 1/2 Fat.

Naomi
Pumpkin Chiffon Pie

Line pie plate with ginger snaps
Filling: 1 cup canned pumpkin
3 eggs, separated
1/2 cups white sugar
1 cup milk
1/2 teaspoon salt
1/2 teaspoon ginger
1/2 teaspoon nutmeg
1 teaspoon cinnamon
2 tablespoons melted butter
1 tablespoon gelatin
1/4 cup cold water
1/2 cup sugar

Cook pumpkin in double boiler 10 mins.
stirring occasionally. Mix egg yolks, sugar and
milk. Add to pumpkin with salt, spices and
melted butter. Stir and cook until custard
consistency. Remove from heat, add gelatin
and water. Chill. When it begins to stiffen, fold
in beaten egg whites to which 1/2 cup sugar
has been added. Pour into ginger snap crust
and chill.
Yield: 1 pie

Naomi
Nut Cracker Pie

Beat 3 egg whites stiff.
Gradually beat in 1 cup sugar.

Crush 12 small soda crackers
Add 1 teaspoon baking powder
1 teaspoon vanilla
3/4 cups chopped nuts

Add these to the egg whites and bake at 350
for 30 mins.

Prepare the two pie shells. Combine
eggs, sugar, salt and spices and beat well.
Blend in canned pumpkin. Add milk and beat
well. Pour into pastry lined pans. Bake at
450^0 for 10 min, then reduce heat and bake
350^0 for 40-45 min.
Yield: 1 pie

Deserts

_____

_____

_____

_____

_____

_____

_____

_____

Naomi
Apple Dessert

1/4 cup oatmeal
1/4 cup flour
1/4 cup brown sugar
1/4 cup shortening (or less)

Put over sliced, sweetened apples and
bake.

Yield: 4 servings

Per Serving (excluding unknown items):
54 Calories; Trace Fat (5.2% calories from fat);
1g Protein; 12g Carbohydrate; 1g Dietary Fiber; 0rng
Cholesterol; 4mg Sodium. Exchanges: 0 Grain
(Starch); 0 Fat; 1/2 Other Carbohydrates.

Naomi
Peppermint Bon Bon

2/3 cup butter
2 cups powdered sugar
3 egg yolks
2 squares melted chocolate
1/2 cup nuts
1 smidgen vanilla
3 egg whites

Whip egg whites and fold in other
ingredients. Butter 13" x 9" pan and crush
vanilla wafers over bottom. Pour the
above mixture over these. Put 2 quarts of
peppermint ice cream (softened) over the
top. Sprinkle more crushed vanilla wafers
over top and freeze.
Yield: 24 servings
Per Serving (excluding unknown items):
167 Calories; 11g Fat (56.9% calories from fat);
2g Protein; 17g Carbohydrate; 1g Dietary Fiber; 40mg
Cholesterol; 62mg Sodium. Exchanges:
0 Grain (Starch); 0 Lean Meat; 2 Fat;
1 Other Carbohydrates.

Naomi
Graham Cracker Dessert

1/2 cup milk
1/2 cup sugar
2 egg yolks, beaten
1 tablespoon unflavored gelatin, dissolve in a
little cold water
1 cup cream, whipped
2 egg whites, beaten
1 dash vanilla

Crumb Mixture
3 tablespoons butter, melted
3 tablespoons brown sugar
12 graham crackers, rolled

Mix milk, sugar and egg yolks and bring to
a boil. Add gelatin and cool. Fold in
whipped cream, egg whites and vanilla. Put
layer of crumbs on top and bottom.
Yield: 12 servings
Per Serving (excluding unknown items):
134 Calories; 9g Fat (59.7% calories from fat);
2g Protein; 12g Carbohydrate; 0g Dietary Fiber, 62mg
Cholesterol; 53mg Sodium. 0 Lean Meat;
0 Non-Fat Milk; 2 Fat.

Naomi
Dessert

2 cans fruit pie mix
1 box white cake mix
1/2 cup butter, melted
1/2 cup nuts, chopped

Spread pie mix in large cake pan. Sprinkle cake mix over it. Pour melted butter over that. Sprinkle with chopped nuts. Bake.
Yield: 20 pieces
Per Serving (excluding unknown items):
139 Calories; 9g Fat (54.3% calories from fat);
1g Protein; 15g Carbohydrate; 1g Dietary Fiber; 12mg Cholesterol; 166mg Sodium. Exchanges:
0 Lean Meat; 1-1/2 Fat; 1 Other Carbohydrates.

Naomi
Crispy Rice Marshmallow Dessert

1/4 cup butter
25 marshmallows
1 18 oz package crispy rice cereal
1 cup coconut, shredded

Melt together butter and marshmallows in top of double boiler. Pour over cereal-coconut mix. Stir. Pack in buttered cake pan.
Yield: 20 squares
Per Serving (excluding unknown items):
159 Calories; 4g Fat (21.7% calories from fat);
2g Protein; 30g Carbohydrate; 1g Dietary Fiber; 6mg Cholesterol; 302mg Sodium. Exchanges:
1 1/2 Grain (Starch); 0 Fruit; 1 Fat; 1/2 Other Carbohydrates.

Naomi
Peanut Butter Crispy Rice Cereal Dessert
From Aunt Phil

1 cup sugar
1 cup white syrup
1 cup peanut butter
6 cups crispy rice cereal

Bring sugar and syrup to a boil. Add
peanut butter and crispy rice cereal and stir.
Press into a large cake pan.

Per Serving (excluding unknown items):
145 Calories; 7g Fat (39.4% calories from fat);
4g Protein; 19g Carbohydrate; 1g Dietary Fiber; 0mg
Cholesterol; 145mg Sodium. Exchanges:
1/2 Grain (Starch); 1/2 Lean Meat; 1 Fat; 1/2 Other
Carbohydrates.

Naomi
Gingerbread

1 cup shortening
1 cup sugar
2 eggs
1 cup molasses
3 cups flour
2 teaspoons cinnamon
1 teaspoon soda
1 pinch salt
1 tablespoon ginger
1 cup water, boiling

Mix all ingredients, except water, well. Now add boiling water. Bake at 375^0 for 25 min. (I bake mine slower & little longer.) Serve with sauce.
SAUCE
1 cup sugar, 1 cup water, lump of butter, grated rind and juice of one lemon and a sprinkling of nutmeg. Thicken with cornstarch to a thin sauce.
Yield: 15 servings
Per Serving (excluding unknown items):
332 Calories; 15g Fat (38.9% calories from fat);
3g Protein; 48g Carbohydrate; 1g Dietary Fiber; 25mg Cholesterol; 26mg Sodium. Exchanges:
1-1/2 Grain (Starch); 0 Lean Meat; 3 Fat; 2 Other Carbohydrates.

Roma
Dandelion Blossom Custard

6 eggs, beaten
1 cup milk
1 teaspoon salt
onion
butter

Pick fresh, yellow dandelion blossoms.
Remove leaves and stems. Wash enough to
fill the bottom of a flat baking dish. Beat
together eggs, milk and salt. Add chopped
onion to taste and pour over dandelion
blossoms. Dot the top with butter and bake at
375^0 until eggs are set.
Serving Ideas: Crumbled bacon can be added
if desired. The dandelions taste like
mushrooms.
Yield: 4 servings
Per Serving (excluding unknown items):
136 Calories; 9g Fat (58.3% calories from fat);
10g Protein; 4g Carbohydrate; 0g Dietary Fiber; 289mg
Cholesterol; 646mg Sodium. Exchanges:
1 Lean Meat; 0 Non-Fat Milk: 1 Fat.

Roma
Angel Fluff Dessert

1/2 cup milk
1/2 cup sugar
2 egg yolks, beaten
1 tablespoon unflavored gelatin, dissolved in cold water
1 cup whipping cream, whipped
2 egg whites, beaten
1 teaspoon vanilla
CRUMB MIX
3 tablespoons butter, melted
3 tablespoons brown sugar
12 graham crackers

Mix milk, sugar and egg yolks and bring to a boil. Add gelatin (dissolved in water). Cool. Fold in whipped cream and beaten egg whites and vanilla. Place in square cake pan and sprinkle with crumb mix. Chill.
Yield: 6 servings
Per Serving (excluding unknown items):
368 Calories; 24g Fat (58.4% calories from fat); 5g Protein; 34g Carbohydrate; Trace Dietary Fiber; 144mg Cholesterol; 191 mg Sodium. Exchanges: 1/2 Grain (Starch); 0 Lean Meat; 0 Non-Fat Milk; 4-1/2 Fat; 1-1/2 Other Carbohydrates.

Roma
Viennese Torte
Very Good and easy.

1 small pkg chocolate chips
1/2 cup butter
1/4 cup water
3 or 4 egg yolks, slightly beaten
2 tablespoons powdered sugar
1 teaspoon vanilla
1-pound cake, store bought or homemade

In a heavy pan, heat chips, butter and water on
med heat stirring until blended. Cool slightly.
Add egg yolks, sugar and vanilla. Stir until
smooth. Chill until spreading consistency, about
45 min. Cut cake into 6 layers, spread
between each layer and assemble into a loaf.
Spread remaining on all sides and top.
Yield: 1 cake
Per Serving (excluding unknown items):
275 Calories; 19g Fat (60.7% calories from fat);
3g Protein; 25g Carbohydrate; 1g Dietary Fiber; 129mg
Cholesterol; 182mg Sodium. Exchanges:
0 Lean Meat; 4 Fat; 1-1/2 Other Carbohydrates.

Roma
Chocolate Dessert

1/2 angel food cake, shredded
2 cups chocolate chips
4 tablespoons sugar
4 egg yolks
4 egg whites
1 pint whipping cream, whipped

Put 1/2 the cake into a large cake pan. Melt the chips, add sugar, egg yolks and cook until thickened. Cool. Beat the egg whites and then beat the whipped cream. Mix with chocolate mixture. Spread 1/2 of this mixture over the shredded cake in the pan. Add rest of cake and rest of chocolate mixture. Serving Ideas: If desired, nuts may be sprinkled over the top and served with a dollop of whipped cream and a cherry on top.

Yield: 1 large cake
Per Serving (excluding unknown items):
336 Calories; 22g Fat (55.5% calories from fat);
5g Protein; 35g Carbohydrate; 2g Dietary Fiber; 100rng Cholesterol; 133mg Sodium. Exchanges:
0 Lean Meat; 0 Non-Fat Milk; 4-1/2 Fat; 2-1/2 Other Carbohydrates.

Roma
Egg-On-Toast Dessert

1 loaf pound cake
1 can apricot halves
whipped cream

Assemble:
Slice of cake, topped with whipped cream and
add 1/2 an apricot (to look like and egg) on
toast.

Naomi
Devil's Food (cheap)

1 cup sugar
1/2 cup lard
2 tablespoons cocoa, in 1/2 cup boiling
water
1 teaspoon soda
1 cup sour milk
2 cups flour
1 pinch salt

Cream together sugar and lard. Put soda in
sour milk. Add all together.
Note the use of lard in so many of
grandma's recipes. She made her own.
Also, the use of sour milk (hence the use of
soda) refrigeration was not all that good
and you didn't throw anything out.
Yield: 12 servings
Per Serving (excluding unknown items):
219 Calories; 9g Fat (36.1 % calories from fat);
2g Protein; 33g Carbohydrate; 1g Dietary Fiber; 8mg
Cholesterol; 12mg Sodium. Exchanges:
1 Grain (Starch); 0 Lean Meat; 1-1/2 Fat;
1 Other Carbohydrates.

Roma
Simple Rum Sauce

1-1/3 cups honey
1/3 cup rum
2/3 cup butter (or margarine)
In a 1-quart saucepan, combine all
ingredients.
Cook over low heat, stirring often, until butter
is melted.
Serving Ideas: Serve warm over ice cream.
Store in refrigerator up to 2 months or in
freezer up to 6 months.
Yield: 2 cups
Per Serving (excluding unknown items):
1545 Calories; 0g Fat (0.0% calories from fat);
1g Protein; 372g Carbohydrate; 1g Dietary Fiber; 0mg
Cholesterol; 19mg Sodium. Exchanges:
25
Other Carbohydrates.

Roma
Caramel Pecan Sauce

1/3 cup butter
1/2 cup sugar
1 cup white syrup
1 egg
1 tablespoon vanilla
1 cup pecans, toasted and chopped

In 1-quart saucepan, combine all ingredients, except pecans. Cook over medium heat, stirring constantly, until mixture comes to a boil (6-8 min). Just before serving, stir in pecans. Serving Ideas: Serve warm over ice cream.

Yield: 2 cups
Per Serving (excluding unknown items):
1752 Calories: 139g Fat (69.3% calories from fat); 15g Protein; 124g Carbohydrate:
8g Dietary Fiber; 353mg Cholesterol;
682mg Sodium. Exchanges: 1-1/2 Grain (Starch); 1-1/2 Lean Meat; 26-1/2 Fat; 6-1/2 Other Carbohydrates.

Roma
Minted Fudge Sauce

1/2 cup sugar
1/4 cup butter
1/3 cup water
2 tablespoons white syrup
1 cup chocolate chips
2 tablespoons creme de menthe (or other favorite liqueur)

In a 1-quart saucepan, combine sugar, butter, water and syrup. Cook over medium heat, stirring constantly, until mixture comes to a full boil (5-8 min). Boil for 3 min. Remove from heat. Immediately add chocolate chips. Beat with a wire whisk until smooth. Stir in liqueur. Serving Ideas: Serve over ice cream or cake.

Yield: 1 112 cups
Per Serving (excluding unknown items):
1862 Calories; 113g Fat (50.1% calories from fat); 10g Protein; 242g Carbohydrate; 13g Dietary Fiber; 124mg Cholesterol; 496mg Sodium. Exchanges:
22-1/2 Fat; 16 Other Carbohydrates.

Roma
Praline Ice Cream Sauce

22 marshmallows
1-1/3 cups brown sugar
1 cup light cream
1 dash salt
4 tablespoons butter
1 teaspoon vanilla
1/3 cup broken pecans

Combine first four ingredients in a 2-1/2-quart saucepan. Heat and stir until mixture comes to a boil. Cook over medium heat about 10 minutes (224^0). Remove from heat; add butter. Cool slightly, add vanilla and nuts. Serve warm.

Yield: 2 cups
Per Serving (excluding unknown items):
2119 Calories; 93g Fat (38.2% calories from fat); 10g Protein; 327g Carbohydrate; 0g Dietary Fiber; 283mg Cholesterol; 980mg Sodium. Exchanges: 18- 1/2 Fat; 21/1/2 Other Carbohydrates.

Roma
Chocolate Ice Cream Sauce

1 package chocolate pudding mix, cooked
not instant
3/4 cup sugar
1-1/2 cups water
2 tablespoons butter

Mix pudding mix, sugar and water in a sauce pan. Cook and stir over low heat until mixture comes to a FULL boil. Remove from heat. Stir in butter. Serving ideas: Serve warm or cold over ice cream or cake.

Yield: 2 1/4 cups
Per Serving (excluding unknown items):
1155 Calories; 25g Fat (18.8% calories from fat);
3g Protein; 241g Carbohydrate; 2g Dietary Fiber; 63mg Cholesterol; 609mg Sodium. Exchanges:
5 Fat; 16 Other Carbohydrates.

Naomi
Freezing Apples
Great for pies

Peel and core apples, quarter them. Drop into
salt solution of 2 tablespoons of salt to a
gallon of water in a glass container or crock.
Do not use aluminum. Let stand, drain and
package. Freeze.
Per Serving (excluding unknown items): 0 Calories; 0g
Fat (0.0% calories from fat); 0g Protein:
0g Carbohydrate; 0g Dietary Fiber;
0rng Cholesterol; 0rng Sodium. Exchanges:

Roma
Kahlua

4 cups water, hot
4 cups sugar
2 tablespoons instant coffee
1 vanilla bean
I fifth cheap bourbon

Dissolve sugar in hot water. Mix with the rest of the ingredients. Let sit for a month.

Per Serving (excluding unknown items):
3097 Calories; 0g Fat (0.0% calories from fat); Trace Protein; 799g Carbohydrate; 0g Dietary Fiber; 0rng Cholesterol; 37mg Sodium. Exchanges: 53-1/2 Other Carbohydrates.

Roma
Rhubarb Wine

1 gallon of boiling water
2 quarts diced rhubarb
3 pounds sugar
1/2 yeast cake
1 pound of raisins
2 lemons

Pour boiling water over the rhubarb and cover tightly. Place a cloth over the crock and let the mixture stand 24 hrs. Strain and reheat. Add sugar, raisins and sliced lemons. When lukewarm, add the yeast. Dissolved in a little water, stirring well. Keep covered for four weeks. Stir often. After fermenting has stopped, strain and filter. Then place in bottles and seal.

Yield: 1 gallon
Per Serving (excluding unknown items):
1599 Calories; 4g Fat (2.2% calories from fat);
25g Protein; 417g Carbohydrate; 38g Dietary Fiber;
0mg Cholesterol; 213mg Sodium. Exchanges:
0 Grain (Starch); 0 Lean Meat; 27 Fruit.

Cookies, Candy and Bars

_____

_____

_____

_____

_____

_____

_____

_____

Naomi
Chocolate Chip Cookies

3/4 cup white sugar
3/4 cup brown sugar
1 cup shortening
2-1/2 cups flour
3 eggs
1 teaspoon soda, in 1 tbsp water
1/2 cup chocolate chips
1 teaspoon vanilla
1 srnidgen salt
nuts

Cream together white and brown sugar
with shortening. Add vanilla, soda & water
and eggs. Stir in flour & salt, then add nuts
and chips. Bake in moderate oven 375^0.
Yield: 60 servings
Per Serving (excluding unknown items) 68 Calories; 4g
Fat (54.8% calories from fat); 1g Protein;
7g Carbohydrate; Trace Dietary Fiber,
9mg Cholesterol; 39mg Sodium. Exchanges:
1/2 Grain (Starch); 0 Lean Meat; 1 Fat; 0 Other
Carbohydrates.

Naomi
Ginger Ice Box Cookies

1 cup walnuts
1 cup shortening
2 cups sugar
2 eggs
1/2 cup molasses
3 teaspoons ginger
1 teaspoon soda
1 teaspoon salt
4-1/2 cups flour

Cream shortening, add sugar, eggs and molasses. Sift flour once before measuring. Add other dry ingredients and sift. Mix and Roll. Chill, slice and bake 375^0 10-12 min.

Yield: 48 servings
Per Serving (excluding unknown items)
141 Calories; 6g Fat (38.1 % calories from fat); 2g Protein; 20g Carbohydrate; Trace Dietary Fiber; 8mg Cholesterol; 48mg Sodium. Exchanges: 1/2 Grain (Starch); 0 Lean Meat; 1 Fat; 1/2 Other Carbohydrates.

Naomi
Coconut Macaroons

2 large egg whites
2 cups powdered sugar
1 teaspoon vanilla
3 cups coconut
Line two large baking sheets with
aluminum foil, set aside. In large bowl,
beat egg whites until stiff. Gradually add
sugar and vanilla, beat a few minutes
longer. With rubber spatula fold in
coconut. Drop mixture by teaspoonfuls onto
prepared baking sheets. Set aside
uncovered at room temperature for 1 hour
to dry out slightly. Bake macaroons for 20
min at 325^0 (I find that 15 min is long
enough because they get too brown on the
bottom.) Cool slightly, peel cookies from
foil and place on racks to cool completely.
Yield: 48 servings
Per Serving (excluding unknown items):
38 Calories; 2g Fat (38.3% calories from fat); Trace
Protein; 6g Carbohydrate; Trace Dietary Fiber;
0mg Cholesterol; 3mg Sodium. Exchanges:
0 Lean Meat; 0 Fruit; 1/2 Fat; 1/2 Other

Naomi
Hermits
Grandpa's favorite

2 cups sugar
1 cup lard
1 teaspoon salt
2 eggs
1/2 pound of seeded raisins, ground
1 teaspoon cloves, cinnamon, allspice
1 teaspoon soda, dissolved in 7 tbsp sour
milk
flour, to make hard

Roll dough and cut with a glass. Bake 10
min 350^0.
Yield: 48 servings
Per Serving (excluding unknown items):
87 Calories; 4g Fat (44.8% calories from fat); Trace
Protein; 12g Carbohydrate; Trace Dietary Fiber; 12mg
Cholesterol; 48mg Sodium. Exchanges:
0 Lean Meat; 0 Fruit; 1 Fat; 1/2 Other Carbohydrates.

Naomi
English Cookies

1 cup shortening
1 cup sugar
1 cup brown sugar
1 cup cold coffee
2 cups raisins
3 cups flour
1 teaspoon baking powder
1 teaspoon soda
1 teaspoon nutmeg
1 tablespoon cinnamon
2 eggs
1 teaspoon salt

There are no directions. I guess grandma knew what to do and did not find it necessary to write it down.

Yield: 60 servings
Per Serving (excluding unknown items):
92 Calories; 4g Fat (34.9% calories from fat);
1g Protein; 14g Carbohydrate; Trace Dietary Fiber;
6mg Cholesterol; 47mg Sodium. Exchanges:
1/2 Grain (Starch); 0 Lean Meat; 1/2 Fruit; 1/2 Fat; 1/2
Other Carbohydrates.

Naomi
Butter Cookies

1 cup sugar
1 cup raisins
1/2 teaspoon salt
2 eggs
3 cups flour
2 teaspoons cream of tartar
1 teaspoon soda
1 teaspoon vanilla

There are no directions. This recipe came from Mrs. Salchert (lived in Grandma's apartment.) She was really old, 65.
Yield: 60 servings
Per Serving (excluding unknown items):
38 Calories; Trace Fat (4.9% calories from fat);
1g Protein; 8g Carbohydrate; Trace Dietary Fiber; 6mg Cholesterol; 20mg Sodium. Exchanges:
1/2 Grain (Starch); 0 Lean Meat; 0 Fruit; 0 Fat;
0 Other Carbohydrates.

Naomi
Million Dollar Cookies

1 cup shortening
1/2 cup white sugar
1/2 cup brown sugar
1 egg
1 teaspoon vanilla
5 -1/4 cups flour
1/2 teaspoon soda
1/2 teaspoon salt
1/2 cup nuts

Cream shortening, sugar, egg and vanilla. Add dry ingredients and nuts. Roll into walnut size balls. Flatten with a glass dipped in sugar. Bake at 375^0

Yield: 48 servings
Per Serving (excluding unknown items):
104 Calories; 5g Fat (46.1 % calories from fat);
2g Protein; 12g Carbohydrate; 1g Dietary Fiber; 4mg Cholesterol; 24mg Sodium. Exchanges:
1/2 Grain (Starch); 0 Lean Meat; 1 Fat;
0 Other Carbohydrates

Naomi
Filled Cookies

1 cup shortening
1 cup sugar
1 egg
1/2 cup milk
1 teaspoon soda
1 teaspoon vanilla
2 teaspoons cream of tartar
3-1/2 cups flour

Filling
1 cup dates
1/2 cup raisins
3/4 cup sugar
1/2 cup water

Boil filling until thick. Here again that's all
of the instructions.
Yield: 48 servings
Per Serving (excluding unknown items):
117 Calories; 5g Fat (34.3% calories from fat);
1g Protein; 18g Carbohydrate; 1g Dietary Fiber; 4mg
Cholesterol; 3mg Sodium. Exchanges: 1/2 Grain
(Starch); 0 Lean Meat; 1/2 Fruit; 0 Non-Fat Milk; 1 Fat;
1/2 Other Carbohydrates.

Naomi
Peanut Ice Box Cookies

1 cup white sugar

1 cup brown sugar

1 cup butter & lard mixed

2 eggs

1 teaspoon soda, in 1/4 c warm water

1 teaspoon baking powder

4 cups flour

1/3 cup peanuts

Mix all together, form a roll-slice and bake

Yield: 60 cookies
Per Serving (excluding unknown items):
180 Calories; 12g Fat (57.9% calories from fat);
7g Protein; 13g Carbohydrate: 2g Dietary Fiber; 6mg
Cholesterol; 15mg Sodium. Exchanges:
1/2 Grain (Starch); 1 Lean Meat; 2 Fat; 0 Other
Carbohydrates.

Naomi
Oatmeal Cookies

1 cup raisins
1-1/2 cups water
1 teaspoon soda
1 cup shortening
1 cup sugar
2 eggs
2 cups oatmeal
2 cups flour
1/2 teaspoon salt

Combine raisins and water and boil 5 min. Drain. Measure 5 tbsp of this liquid and combine with soda. Cream shortening, sugar and eggs. Add oatmeal, salt and raisins. Add soda mixture. Stir in flour. Drop on cookie sheet. Bake at 350^0 10 min. (Add nuts, if preferred)

Yield: 60 cookies
Per Serving (excluding unknown items):
78 Calories; 4g Fat (42.8% calories from fat);
1g Protein; 10g Carbohydrate; 1g Dietary Fiber; 6mg Cholesterol; 20mg Sodium. Exchanges:
1/2 Grain (Starch); 0 Lean Meat; 0 Fruit; 1/2 Fat;
0 Other Carbohydrates.

Roma
Peanut Butter Cookies
1 cup peanut butter
1 cup sugar (or sugar substitute)
1 teaspoon vanilla
1 egg yolk
1 egg white, beaten until stiff

Combine first four ingredients, fold in egg whites. Roll into small balls and press with a fork on ungreased cookie sheet. Bake 10-12 min at 325^0.

Three Ingredient Fudge

3 cups semisweet chocolate chips
1 (14 ounce) can sweetened condensed milk
1/4 cup butter
Optional mix-ins: walnuts, candy, pretzels, etc.

Add semi-sweet chocolate chips, sweetened condensed milk, and butter in large microwaveable bowl. Warm in microwave on medium until melted, about 3-5 minute. Be sure to stir about every minute.
Pour fudge mixture into well-greased 8x8-inch glass baking dish. Refrigerate until set.
Enjoy! Yes, sometimes ENJOY needs its own step in the directions.

Naomi
Orange Refrigerator Cookies

2-1/2 cups flour
1/2 teaspoon salt
1/4 teaspoon soda
1/2 teaspoon baking powder
1/2 cup shortening, softened
1/2 cup butter
1/2 cup brown sugar, firmly packed
1/2 cup white sugar
1 egg, unbeaten
2 tablespoons orange juice
1 tablespoon grated/orange rind
1 teaspoon lemon extract
1 cup nuts

Bake 12 mins at 350^0.

Naomi
Candy

2 packages caramel chips
1 package chocolate chips

Melt in double boiler over hot water. Stir
in 1 can chow mein noodles and 1 cup
salted nuts. Drop on buttered platter.

I have no idea what caramel chips are,
perhaps butterscotch. But it sounds like an
easy recipe. Mom
Yield: 48 servings
Per Serving (excluding unknown items):
22 Calories; 1g Fat (49.7% calories from fat); Trace
Protein: 3g Carbohydrate; Trace Dietary Fiber;
0mg Cholesterol; 1 mg Sodium. Exchanges:
1/2 Fat; 0 Other Carbohydrates.

Naomi
English Toffee

1 cup sugar
1/2 pound of butter
1/4 cup water

Melt butter with water. Add sugar. Stir
constantly until it is a rich brown color.
Remove from fire and pour over finely
chopped nuts. Let harden and frost with
melted sweet chocolate. Break into pieces.
Yield: 24 servings
Per Serving (excluding unknown items):
68 Calories; 8g Fat (99.5% calories from fat); Trace
Protein; Trace Carbohydrate: 0g Dietary Fiber, 21mg
Cholesterol; 78mg Sodium.
Exchanges: 1-1/2 Fat.

Naomi
Seafoam Candy
A lot like divinity

2 cups sugar
1/2 cup white corn syrup
1/2 cup water
2 egg whites
1 cup nutmeats, chopped
1 teaspoon vanilla

Boil sugar, syrup and water until mixture dropped in cold water turns brittle. Pour slowly over stiffly beaten whites of eggs. Add nuts and vanilla. Beat until mixture is creamy. Pour on buttered platter or dish.

Yield: 24 servings
Per Serving (excluding unknown items):
65 Calories; 0g Fat (0.0% calories from fat);
0g Protein; 17g Carbohydrate: 0g Dietary Fiber; 0mg Cholesterol; Trace Sodium. Exchanges:
1 Other Carbohydrates.

Naomi
Velvet Fudge

3 squares unsweetened chocolate
3 cups sugar
1 cup evaporated milk
3 tablespoons butter
1 teaspoon vanilla

Cut chocolate over sugar into a 2 quart saucepan. Add syrup and milk. Place over medium heat, stirring until sugar dissolves and chocolate melts. Bring to boiling, cover and cook 2 min. Uncover and cook, stirring occasionally to 234^0 or until softball forms when a small amount is dropped into cold water. Remove from heat. Add butter and let cool, stirring until mixture is 110^0 or pan is cool enough to hold in palm of hand. Add vanilla and beat until thick and no longer glossy. Put in buttered pan. Cut into squares. (Nuts may be added if desired).
Yield: 24 servings
Per Serving (excluding unknown items):
128 Calories; 3g Fat (22.4% calories from fat); Trace Protein; 26g.

Roma
Fudge
The Temp (224^0) the cocoa and beating while hot is what makes this recipe different.

2 cups sugar
2/3 cup milk
5 tablespoons powdered cocoa
2 tablespoons salad oil
2 tablespoons white syrup
1 dash salt
2 tablespoons butter
1 teaspoon vanilla
1/2 cup chopped nuts, optional

Combine cocoa and oil. Combine milk, syrup and salt in heavy saucepan. Add cocoa mixture. Bring to a rolling boil and add sugar. Stir until mixture returns to a boil. Let boil, without stirring, to 224^0. Remove from heat, DO NOT COOL! Add butter and vanilla and beat on high speed 4-6 min or until thick and loses its gloss. Add nuts if desired. Put into buttered container or platter.
Per Serving (excluding unknown items):
2543 Calories; 96g Fat (32.8% calories from fat); 17g Protein; 424g Carbohydrate; 7g

Roma
Divinity
Make this every Christmas

4 cups sugar
1 cup light corn syrup
3/4 cup water
3 egg whites, stiffly beaten
1 teaspoon vanilla
1 cup nuts, chopped

Mix sugar, corn syrup and water in heavy saucepan. Stir over low heat until sugar is dissolved; then cook without stirring to 255^0 (hard ball). Remove from heat and pour, beating constantly, in a fine stream into beaten egg whites. Add vanilla and continue beating until mixture holds its shape and becomes slightly dull. Fold in nuts. Drop quickly from tip of buttered spoon onto waxed paper in individual peaks.
Yield: 60 pieces
Per Serving (excluding unknown items):
83 Calories: 1g Fat (13.9% calories from fat);
1g Protein; 18g Carbohydrate; Trace Dietary Fiber;
0mg Cholesterol; 10mg Sodium. Exchanges:
0 Grain (Starch); 0 Lean Meat; 0 Fat; 1 Other Carbohydrates.

Roma
Fudge Bars

1 stick butter or margarine
1 cup sugar
4 eggs
1 teaspoon vanilla
1 large can chocolate syrup
1 cup flour
1 pinch salt
1/2 cup nuts

Cream together butter and sugar. Add eggs, vanilla and chocolate syrup. Stir in flour and salt and nuts. Bake at 350^0 for 40-45 min.

Yield: 16 servings
Per Serving (excluding unknown items):
172 Calories; 9g Fat (48.4% calories from fat);
3g Protein; 20g Carbohydrate; 1g Dietary Fiber; 62mg
Cholesterol; 81mg Sodium. Exchanges:
1/2 Grain (Starch); 1/2 Lean Meat; 1-1/2 Fat;
1 Other Carbohydrates.

Mildred
Mrs. Eisenhower's Fudge

4-1/2 cups sugar
1 tall can evaporated milk
1 pinch salt
2 tablespoons butter
12 ounces chocolate chips
12 ounces German chocolate cake mix
1-pint marshmallow creme
2 cups nuts, chopped
1 dash vanilla

Mix sugar, milk and salt together and boil for 6 mins. Add butter. Put chocolate chips, German chocolate, marshmallow, nuts and vanilla into large bowl. Pour hot syrup over and beat until melted. Pour into buttered cake pan (13" x 9"). Cut into squares when cool. It's better if kept refrigerated.

Yield: 60 servings
Per Serving (excluding unknown items):
146 Calories; 6g Fat (32.5% calories from fat);
2g Protein; 25g Carbohydrate; 1g Dietary Fiber; 2mg Cholesterol; 48mg Sodium. Exchanges:
0 Grain (Starch); 0 Lean Meat; 0 Non-Fat Milk;
1 Fat; 1-1/2 Other Carbohydrates.

Roma
French Fudge
YUM!!

1 package chocolate chips
1/3 cup + 1 tbsp sweetened condensed milk
1 pinch salt
1/2 Teaspoon vanilla

Melt chocolate, without stirring, in top of double boiler over rapidly boiling water. Remove from heat. Add condensed milk, salt and vanilla. Stir only until blended. Turn into container lined with waxed paper and press into block about I" thick. Chill until firm. Turn out of container and cut into serving pieces. Store in airtight container.
Yield: 1/2 pound or 20 servings
Per Serving (excluding unknown items):
70 Calories; 4g Fat (44.0% calories from fat);
1g Protein; 10g Carbohydrate: 1g Dietary Fiber; 2mg Cholesterol; 14mg Sodium. Exchanges:
1 Fat; 1/2 Other Carbohydrates.

Roma
Potato Candy
Tastes like Mound Bars

4 cups powdered sugar
2 cups coconut
3/4 cup mashed potatoes (without milk
and butter added), cold
1-1/2 teaspoons vanilla,
1/2 teaspoon salt
1-pound chocolate candy coating

In a large bowl, combine sugar, coconut, potatoes, vanilla and salt. Mix well. Line a 9" square pan with foil; butter foil. Spread coconut mixture into pan. Cover and refrigerate overnight. Cut into 2" x 1" rectangles. Cover and freeze. In a double boiler, melt candy coating. Dip bars into coating; place on waxed paper to harden. Store in airtight container.

Yield: 2 pounds
Per Serving (excluding unknown items):
2453 Calories; 54g Fat (19.3% calories from fat);
5g Protein; 504g Carbohydrate; 14g Dietary Fiber; 0mg
Cholesterol; 1103mg Sodium. Exchanges:
1-1/2 Fruit; 10-1/2 Fat; 32 Other carbohydrates.

Roma
Toffee

1 cup pecans, chopped
3/4 cup brown sugar, packed
1/2 cup butter
1/2 cup semi-sweet chocolate chips

Sprinkle pecans on bottom of buttered
9"x 9" pan. Combine sugar and butter in
saucepan. Bring to a boil, stirring constantly,
7 min. Remove from heat and spread over
nuts. Sprinkle chips over top. Cover pan so
heat will melt chocolate. Spread evenly over
top. Cut into squares while still warm.
Refrigerate to set.

Yield: 36 pieces
Per Serving (excluding unknown items):
69 Calories; 6g Fat (67.9% calories from fat); Trace
Protein; 5g Carbohydrate; Trace Dietary Fiber;
7mg Cholesterol; 28mg Sodium. Exchanges:
0 Grain (Starch); 0 Lean Meat; 1 Fat;
1/2 Other Carbohydrates.

Roma
Lemon-Butter Snowbars

Crust
1/2 cup butter, softened
1/3 cup flour
1/4 cup sugar
Filling
2 eggs
3/4 cup sugar
2 tablespoons flour
1/4 teaspoon baking powder
3 tablespoons lemon juice
confectioner's sugar

Preheat Oven to 350^0. In small mixer bowl combine crust ingredients. Mix on low speed until blended (1 min). Pat into ungreased 8" square baking pan. Bake for 15-20 min or until brown around the edges. Meanwhile, prepare filling. Combine all filling ingredients and blend well. Pour filling over partially baked crust. Return to oven for 18-20 min longer or until set. Sprinkle with confectioner's, sugar. Cool.
Yield: 16 servings
Per Serving (excluding unknown items):
121 Calories; 6g Fat (46.1% calories from fat);
1g Protein; 16g Carbohydrate; Trace

Roma
Snicker Bars

1 cup milk chocolate chips
1/4 cup butterscotch chips
1/4 cup creamy peanut butter
FILLING
1/4 cup butter
1 cup sugar
1/4 cup evaporated milk
1-1/2 cups marshmallow creme
1/4 cup creamy peanut butter
1 teaspoon vanilla
1-1/2 cups salted peanuts, chopped
CARAMEL LAYER
1 package 14oz caramels
1/4 cup whipping cream
ICING
1 cup milk chocolate chips
1/4 cup butterscotch chips
1/4 cup creamy peanut butter

Line a 13" x 9" x 2" pan with foil. Butter the foil and set aside. Combine the first three ingredients in a small saucepan. Stir over low heat until melted and smooth. Spread into prepared pan. Chill until set. For filling, melt the butter in a heavy saucepan over medium heat. Add sugar and milk. Bring to a gentle boil. Reduce heat to medium-low. Boil and stir for 5 min. Remove from heat. Stir in marshmallow creme, peanut butter and vanilla. Add peanuts. Spread over first layer. Chill until set. Combine caramels and cream in a saucepan. Stir over low heat until melted and smooth. Cook and stir 4 min longer. Spread over second layer. Chill until set. In another saucepan, combine chips and peanut butter. Stir over low heat until melted and smooth. Pour over the caramel layer. Chill at least 4 hrs. Remove from refrigerator 20 min before cutting. Remove from the pan. Cut into 1" squares.

Yield: 96 pieces

Per Serving (excluding unknown items):
37 Calories; 2g Fat (43.7% calories from fat); Trace Protein; 5g Carbohydrate; Trace Dietary Fiber; 3mg Cholesterol; 9mg Sodium. Exchanges: 0 Non-Fat Milk; 1/2 Fat; 1/2 Other carbohydrates.

Roma
Peanut Brittle

3 cups sugar
1/2 cup light corn syrup
1-1/3 cups water
13 ounces salted peanuts
2 tablespoons butter
1/2 teaspoon soda

Lightly butter two large cookie sheets.
Combine sugar, corn syrup and water in a heavy large saucepan. Heat over medium heat, stirring constantly, until sugar dissolves, then cook, without stirring, to 270^0. Sprinkle peanuts into syrup mixture and add butter, but do not stir in. Continue cooking to 300^0. Remove from heat. Dissolve soda in 2 teaspoons water in a cup. Stir into syrup mixture. Let stand a few minutes until foaming almost stops. Pour onto cookie sheets; quickly spread as thin as possible with a spatula. Let stand until cool and firm. Break into bite-size pieces. Store in a tightly covered container.
Yield: 3 pounds
Per Serving (excluding unknown items):
2988 Calories; 23g Fat (6.7% calories from fat); Trace Protein: 725g Carbohydrate; 0g Dietary Fiber;
62mg Cholesterol; 448mg Sodium. Exchanges: 4-1/2 Fat;
48-1/2 Other Carbohydrates.

Roma
2-4-6
Remember?

2 butter
4 white syrup
6 sugar
Chocolate chips, optional

Use any kind of a measure you want. Just use the above ratio. Mix and boil until sugar is melted. (At least one minute in the microwave.) If you want chocolate flavor, stir in chocolate chips after you remove from microwave. This makes delicious caramel candy or ice cream topping.
Nuts can be added if desired
Per Serving (excluding unknown items):
6270 Calories; 184g Fat (25.6% calories from fat); 2g Protein; 1199g Carbohydrate; 0g Dietary Fiber; 497mg Cholesterol; 1885mg Sodium. Exchanges: 36-1/2 Fat; 80-1/2 Other Carbohydrates.

Naomi
Granola

4 cups oatmeal
1/2 cup wheat germ
1 cup pecans (or other nuts)
1 cup raisins
1 tablespoon brewer's yeast
3 tablespoons powdered milk
2 tablespoons granular lecithin
1/4 cup maple syrup
1/4 cup oil
1 tablespoon vanilla

Heat oven to 375°. Toast oatmeal until lightly browned in roasting pan (about 20 min. Stir every 5 min). Add remaining ingredients and mix well. Return to oven another 15-20 min, stirring every 5 min.

Yield: 6 1/2 cups
Per Serving (excluding unknown items):
228 Calories; 7g Fat (28.2% calories from fat);
6g Protein; 36g Carbohydrate; 4g Dietary Fiber; 2mg Cholesterol; 11 mg Sodium. Exchanges:
1-1/2 Grain (Starch); 1/2 Fruit; 0 Non-Fat Milk;
1-1/2 Fat; 1/2 Other Carbohydrates

Pickles

_____

_____

_____

_____

_____

_____

_____

_____

Naomi
Sliced Sweet Pickles

7 cups cucumbers, sliced
1 cup green peppers, sliced
1 cup onion, chopped
2 tablespoons salt
1 tablespoon celery seed or mustard seed
1 cup vinegar
2 cups sugar

Mix vegetables with salt and seeds. Mix vinegar and sugar to dissolve. Pour over vegetables. Pack in jars and refrigerate. Let stand 24 hrs before use. Will keep for weeks in refrigerator

Yield: 2 quarts
Per Serving (excluding unknown items):
1777 Calories; 1g Fat (0.7% calories from fat);
8g Protein; 457g Carbohydrate; 11g Dietary Fiber. 0mg Cholesterol; 12819mg Sodium. Exchanges:
8 Vegetable; 28 Other Carbohydrates.

Mildred
Dill Pickles
THESE ARE THE BEST

1 peck of small cucumbers
3 quarts vinegar
3 quarts water
1-1/2 cups sugar
1-1/2 cups salt, not iodized
1-1/2 tablespoons powdered alum
fresh dill

Pack pickles in jars with dill. Make a hot syrup
out of other ingredients and cover the
cucumbers. Seal.

Yield: 8 quarts
Per Serving (excluding unknown items):
1564 Calories; 0g Fat (0.0% calories from fat);
0g Protein; 470g Carbohydrate; 0g Dietary Fiber; 0mg
Cholesterol; 153599mg Sodium. Exchanges: 31-1/2
Other Carbohydrates.

Naomi
Pickled Beets
The only way to eat beets

3 cups water
1 cup sugar
1 cup vinegar

Bring to a boil, add peeled beets and put in
Jars.
Yield: 2 quarts
Per Serving (excluding unknown items):
808 Calories; 0g Fat (0.0% calories from fat);
0g Protein; 214g Carbohydrate; 0g Dietary Fiber; 0rng
Cholesterol; 26mg Sodium. Exchanges:
14-1/2 Other Carbohydrates.

Naomi
Cranberry Relish

1 pound of fresh cranberries
2 oranges (rind of one)
2 apples
3 cups sugar

Mix and serve
Serving Ideas: May add some nuts, if desired
Yield: 8 servings
Per Serving (excluding unknown items):
338 Calories; Trace Fat (0.6% calories from fat); Trace
Protein; 87g Carbohydrate; 3g Dietary Fiber; 0mg
Cholesterol; 1mg Sodium. Exchanges: 1 Fruit; 5 Other
Carbohydrates.

Naomi
Pickle Relish

Grind cucumbers, onion and salt and let
stand. Heat equal parts vinegar and sugar.
Add a smidgen of celery seed and mustard
seed. Can.
Per Serving (excluding unknown items): 0 Calories; 0g
Fat (0.0% calories from fat); 0g Protein;
0g Carbohydrate; 0g Dietary Fiber;
0mg Cholesterol; 0mg Sodium. Exchanges: .

Naomi
Pickled Fish
Makes Northern Pike taste like Pickled
Herring

2 cups white vinegar
1 cup sugar
1/2 cup dry white wine
2 bay leaves
1/2 teaspoon whole allspice
2 teaspoons whole mustard seed
4 whole cloves
1/2 teaspoon black pepper, coarsely ground

Bring all ingredients to a boil for a few min.
Cool. Put cut-up fish (not necessary to de-
bone), lots of onion and 1/4 lemon in a jar and
pour syrup over (to fill jar). Refrigerate at least
3-4 days. Serving Ideas: Good on a ritz.
Per Serving (excluding unknown items):
1045 Calories; 8g Fat (6.3% calories from fat);
4g Protein; 249g Carbohydrate; 10g Dietary Fiber; 0mg
Cholesterol; 78mg Sodium. Exchanges:
1-1/2 Grain (Starch); 0 Lean Meat; 1-1/2 Fat;
15-1/2 Other Carbohydrates.

Naomi
Bread and Butter Pickles

1 cup sugar
1 cup vinegar
1 tablespoon pickling spices
1 onion
1 tablespoon salt
several cucumbers

Slice cucumbers and onions. Let stand in
saltwater over night. Drain. Bring sugar,
vinegar and spices to a boil. Drop in pickles.
Cook about 15 min.

Yield: I quart
Per Serving (excluding unknown items):
849 Calories; Trace Fat (0.2% calories from fat);
1g Protein; 223g Carbohydrate; 2g Dietary Fiber; 0rng
Cholesterol; 6403mg Sodium. Exchanges:
1-1/2 Vegetable; 14-1/2 Other Carbohydrates.

Miscellaneous

_____

_____

_____

_____

_____

_____

_____

_____

Naomi
Grandma's Lye Soap
Not for ears

9 Cups lard
11 cups cold water
1 box lye
4 tablespoons borax
1 dab citronella

Melt lard, dissolve borax, add lye. Stir slowly
until it looks like honey. Let set.

Roma
Furniture Polish
Good and cheap

Shake in a jar equal parts of boiled linseed oil, white vinegar and turpentine. (Gets milky). Saturate cloth and rub in. Wipe with clean soft cloth.

Household Uses for Vinegar

Cleaning drains: Pour 1/2 cup baking soda in the drain, followed by 1/2 cup vinegar; the mixture will foam as it cleans and deodorizes. Use every few weeks to keep drains clean.

Mildew on plastic shower curtains: Put the shower curtain in the washing machine with light-colored towels; add 1 cup white vinegar to the detergent and wash.

Soap scum on shower: Spray on vinegar, scrub and rinse.

Toilet hard-water rings: Shut off water at the tank and flush to remove as much water as possible. Spray vinegar on the ring, sprinkle in borax and scrub with drywall sandpaper.

Shower head deposits: Pour white vinegar into a plastic bag, tape to the shower head and leave overnight. Brush the shower head to remove remaining deposits.

Softening laundry: Fill dispenser with 1/4 cup white vinegar to soften laundry without leaving odors.

Cleaning vinyl floors: Add 1/4 cup vinegar to 1-gallon hot water for spotless floors.

Cleaning windows: Mix 50 percent white vinegar with 50 percent water in a spray bottle. Spray glass surfaces and wipe dry.

Neutralize pet odors: Mix 1-part white vinegar to 3 parts water. Pour on stained areas and blot; never rub to remove stains and odors.

Greasy dishes: Mix 2 tablespoons white vinegar to liquid dish soap to boost its cleaning power.

Baking Soda things, you can look up on the internet.

Baking Soda Uses for Cleaning
- Clean Your Bathtub
- Deodorize Your Refrigerator
- Clean and Unclog Drains
- Add to the Dishwasher or Use as a Cleaner in the Bathroom
- Extinguish Grease Fires
- Deodorize Shoes
- Closet Freshener
- Deodorize the Cat Box
- Deodorize Your Cutting Boards
- Deodorize Trashcans
- Clean the Inside of Your Dishwasher
- Deodorize Garbage Disposals
- Deodorize Recycling Bin
- Deodorize Kid's Lunch Boxes
- Deodorize Carpets and Clean a Mattress
- Clean the Pool

Baking Soda Benefits for Health

- Natural Deodorant
- Face Exfoliator
- Hand Softener
- Soothe Tired Feet
- Relieve Itchy Skin
- Remove Splinters
- Clean Your Hair Brush and Wig
- Clean Your Hair with Baking Soda
- Soothe Bug Bites
- Relieve a Sunburn
- Clean Your Teeth with Homemade Baking Soda Toothpaste
- Whiten Your Teeth
- Freshen Your Mouth and Heal Canker Sore Faster
- Enhance Your Exercise
- Improve Kidney Function
- Reduce Ulcer Pain

HOUSEHOLD USES FOR LEMONS

- **For Health**
- For a sore throat or bad breath, gargle with some lemon juice.
- After a shampoo, rinse your hair with lemon juice to make it shine. Mix the strained juice of a lemon in an eight-ounce glass of warm water.
- Suck on a lemon to settle an upset stomach.
- **In the Kitchen**
- Clean discolored utensils with a cloth dipped in lemon juice. Rinse with warm water.
- Toss used lemons into your garbage disposal to help keep it clean and smelling fresh.
- Use one-part lemon juice and two parts salt to scour chinaware to its original luster.
- Rub kitchen and bathroom faucets with lemon peel. Wash and dry with a soft cloth to shine and remove spots.
- Fresh lemon juice in rinse water removes soap film from interiors of ovens and refrigerators.

- Fish or onion odor on your hands can be removed by rubbing them with fresh lemons.
- To get odors out of wooden rolling pins, bowls, or cutting boards, rub with a piece of lemon. Don't rinse: The wood will absorb the lemon juice.
- Clean copper pots by cutting a lemon in half and rubbing the cut side with salt until the salt sticks. Rub the lemon onto the metal, rinse with hot water, and polish dry.
- **Outdoors**
- Save lemon and orange rinds to deter squirrels and cats from digging in the garden. Store rinds in the freezer during the winter, and then bury them just under the surface of the garden periodically throughout the spring and summer.
- A few drops of lemon juice in outdoor house-paint will keep insects away while you are painting and until the paint dries.
- Mix one tablespoon of lemon juice with two tablespoons of salt to make a rust-removing scrub.

- **Miscellaneous Uses**
- Remove scratches on furniture by mixing equal parts of lemon juice and salad oil and rubbing it on the scratches with a soft cloth.
- To make furniture polish, mix one-part lemon juice and two parts olive oil.
- To clean the surface of white marble or ivory (such as piano keys), rub with a half a lemon, or make a lemon juice and salt paste. Wipe with a clean, wet cloth.
- To renew hardened paintbrushes, dip into boiling lemon juice. Lower the heat and leave the brush for 15 minutes, then wash it in soapy water.
- To remove dried paint from glass, apply hot lemon juice with a soft cloth. Leave until nearly dry, and then wipe off.
- Create your own air freshener: Slice some lemons, cover with water, and let simmer in a pot for about an hour. (This will also clean your aluminum pots!)
- Before you start to vacuum, put a few drops of lemon juice in the dust bag. It will make the house smell fresh.
- Get grimy cotton socks white again by boiling them in water with a slice of lemon.

Made in the USA
Columbia, SC
07 September 2021

45060453R00098